SEEKING

GOD'S

FACE

Practical Reflections on
Honor and *Shame* in *Scripture*

Brad Vaughn and Ryan Jensen

"It's one thing to grasp a concept intellectually. It's another thing to apply it to your heart. Vaughn and Jensen invite their readers to wrestle, prayerfully and personally, with a cultural dynamic unfamiliar to many Western Christians but deeply significant to the characters and first readers of the Bible. The result is a unique blend of scholarly reflection and personal devotion."

Brandon O'Brien, Ph.D., Director of Content Development and Distribution for Redeemer City to City, co-author of *Misreading Scripture with Western Eyes*

"*Seeking God's Face* provides 101 passages across the landscape of Scripture to help dissipate the fog surrounding honor and shame, clearing the way for more genuine worship and works. Read this book with caution because it will touch your heart, head, and hands."

Tom Steffen, DMiss., Professor emeritus, Cook School of Intercultural Studies, Biola University

"In this series of reflections, Brad Vaughn and Ryan Jensen take the reader into the scriptures through the lens of honor and shame. Although this is a perspective often lost to Western readers, it is close to the cultures in which the stories of the Bible are embedded. Thus, they bring out both illuminating and thought-provoking conclusions, while also maintaining a cruciform focus that highlights God's challenge to and care of the church."

Lucy Peppiatt, Ph.D., Principal of Westminster Theological Centre, UK, author of *Rediscovering Scripture's Vision for Women*

"*Seeking God's Face* takes our hearts and minds on a tour through the biblical story, showing us how honor and shame are powerful themes throughout Scripture. It's theologically robust, deeply formative, and accessible to a broad range of readers. This book is a gift to God's people. I highly recommend it."

Jim Mullins, Lead Pastor of Redemption Tempe, co-author of *The Symphony of Mission: Playing Your Part in God's Work in the World*

"*Seeking God's Face* will help you to see the Bible in a new light by bringing out the themes of shame and honor where you didn't see them before. In addition to explaining the meaning of numerous passages in the Old and New Testaments, the book encourages readers to reflect on ways they have shamed God or others, to repent from dishonoring behaviors, and practice honoring God with our lives. These contemplations on a biblical worldview of shame and honor can serve to correct any culture's practices that dishonor others."

Kenneth Nehrbass, Ph.D., Associate professor of Global Studies, Rawlings School of Divinity, Liberty University

"The conversation about honor and shame is complicated—and at times contentious—in contemporary evangelicalism. Some run headlong into adopting honor and shame as cultural categories according to local definitions and customs. Others reject honor and shame altogether fearing that adoption would serve as a harbinger of a loss of objective morality. The problem with these approaches is that both can neglect what the Bible actually has to say about these themes.

What Vaughn and Jensen have done in this helpful devotional is to put the Bible's own discussion of these topics in front of the reader while prompting meaningful, personal reflection and application. Before you make up your mind on the issues, work through this devotional volume and take time to reflect on the Bible's own presentation of these important elements of human existence."

Matthew Bennett, Ph.D., Assistant Professor of
Missions and Theology, Cedarville University

"By interacting with scriptures in both OT and NT, Brad and Ryan have written a helpful and insightful devotional guide for those who want to learn more about honor and shame. As a scholar and pastor from the Majority World, I highly recommend this book to people who struggle with the daily experience of shame."

Patrick Chan, General Secretary,
Hong Kong Campus Crusade for Christ.

"In this volume, Vaughn and Jensen bring a fuller picture and understanding of the honor and shame perspective, by showing how this lens is prevalent in the biblical worldview. Written in a devotional format, it has the breadth of research and careful exegesis that Vaughn is known for. They show that this deeper understanding should then make a difference in our daily lives, our communities, and our relationship with God.

It's recommended for those who are familiar with the subject, for it causes us to pause to reflect more deeply on Scripture as well as for those for whom this may be their first step to understanding this dimension of Scripture."

Kiem-Kiok Kwa, Ph.D., Lecturer,
Biblical Graduate School of Theology, Singapore

"In *Seeking God's Face*, Brad Vaughn and Ryan Jensen dispense the myth that the Bible is confusing, out of date, and inferior to Enlightenment reasoning. This volume offers a grand narrative of 101 scriptural reflections through the lens of honor and shame that reveals a repeated cultural pattern that challenges our biased Western views and nudges us toward new ways of Christian living and growing in our love of the blessed Trinity."

Robert Gallagher, Ph.D., Professor of Intercultural
Studies Emeritus, A. Duane Litfin School of Mission,
Ministry, & Leadership, Wheaton College

"*Seeking God's Face* will inspire new reflections on honor and shame, whether you are a veteran or rookie to this theological discussion. Brad Vaughn and Ryan Jensen offer 101 short reflections on key Bible passages then provide a parting reflection and prayer. I found myself sitting forward in my office chair to absorb their insight and then sitting back to reflect on what it means for my life. The further I went in this book, the more I appreciated the beautiful blend of theological depth and psychological honesty. I recommend *Seeking God's Face* for personal devotion or group study on this important biblical concept."

Chris Sneller, Ph.D., Director of Innovation, Bridges International;
Lecturer in Missional Theology, Houston Baptist University

"My mirror shows the way I dress and appear each time I stand before it. It helps me to see who I am and how others might think about me from the way I look. I may be honored or abased by others based on my appearance. While there are many devotions on the shelves, I recommend *Seeking God's Face* for your spiritual mirror to help you walk in spiritual honor before the Lord and the world in the face of honor and shame."

Haggai Alhamdu Habila, Pastor/Chaplain at
Living Spring Fellowship, Puyallup, WA

"During the past decade living in East Africa, I have grown more aware each passing day of how much I interpret and teach the Scriptures through my Western outlook and understanding. This can limit the scope and impact of cross-cultural ministry in such collectivistic and hospitable cultures like this one. Working each day through *Seeking God's Face* has deepened and enriched both my personal faith and my cross-cultural Bible-teaching ministry by opening up new vistas on familiar Old and New Testament passages.

In their introduction, Brad Vaughn and Ryan Jensen state that they intend this set of 101 reflections to "affect our head, heart, and hands." I can vouch that this is wonderfully true, and thus I recommend this book wholeheartedly for anyone wishing to engage more profoundly with the beauty of God's character and purposes from fresh global perspectives!"

Chris Howles, DIS, Head of Theology Uganda Martyrs Seminary Namugongo. Founder of www.fromeverynation.net

I must confess, I've been new to learning about honor and shame dynamics the last few years. Yet I've had no greater teacher than Brad Vaughn. These dynamics are everywhere in Scripture—and in culture today, blind as we may be to them. *Seeking God's Face* will help you have "eyes to see" these powerful dynamics in the biblical story, in your own life, and in society around you today.

Joshua Butler, Author of *The Skeletons in God's Closet* and *The Pursuing God*

It is my pleasure to recommend *Seeking God's Face: Practical Reflections on Honor and Shame in Scripture*. This collection of essays, based on critical texts from both the Old and the New Testaments, is beautifully devotional in nature. At the same time, *Seeking God's Face* not only provides its readers with critical insights into honor and shame, but it does so in a manner that is easily accessible and useful to pastors, scholars, and lay people. It also demonstrates how a clear understanding of honor and shame can deepen our understanding of important biblical texts, as well as their function within the broader narrative of Scripture. Frankly, I am amazed that the authors have managed to accomplish so much in this delightful, easily readable, work!

Thomas J. Sappington, Th.D., Associate Professor of Intercultural Studies, Biola University

One of today's important discussions is that of taking the gospel into societies, which unlike much of the West, are heavily shaped by honor-shame values. Few resources on this topic exist to equip the Church for such ministry contexts. And those available are often academic in nature and beyond the reach of most believers. Vaughn and Jensen are to be commended on providing the Church with a very helpful, user-friendly work. *Seeking God's Face* is a creative and innovative piece of mission literature. Part Bible study, part devotional, this book takes readers on a journey to understand what the Scriptures have to say about the topics of honor and shame. Part training manual, part practical guide, this book assists readers with making disciples of all nations—particularly the majority who hold honor-shame value systems.

J. D. Payne, Ph.D., Professor of Christian Ministry, Samford University

Contents

— The New Testament —

Introduction

———————— ⑈ ————————

Why Reflect on Honor and Shame in the Bible?

This book originally had no introduction. But as we shared early drafts, people repeatedly asked us to include an introduction that would explain several ideas related to honor and shame. They asked for clear, direct explanations about what we meant by these concepts. Accordingly, this brief introduction is written very differently than the reflections you'll find in the rest of this book.

Although honor and shame are present in all cultures, people's experiences with these concepts may differ. Some people suppose that honor is an outdated concept from the medieval ages; others think honor is a synonym for pride and leads to so-called "honor killings." Likewise, countless readers will assume that shame is wholly bad, a cancer upon the human psyche. In truth, both concepts are richer and more practical than many people imagine.

We've also heard Western Christians attempt to use the Bible to minimize the importance of honor and shame. Westerners often explain sin in legal terms, emphasize guilt, and stress the importance of the individual. This perspective is certainly drawn from the Bible. However, it overlooks another view common throughout the world and ubiquitous in Scripture. For many people, honor and shame are primary concerns. Their concern for their community and their place in it is not peripheral but paramount.

We don't suggest that Western theology is "wrong" or that Westerners don't understand some aspects of honor and shame. Instead, we suggest that Scripture has much more to say to us than we might think. As we read the Bible through the lens of honor and shame, we can grow in our love for God, in Christlikeness, and in wisdom from the Spirit.

Tips for Reading This Book

This book contains 101 reflections on honor and shame from across the pages of Scripture. We purposely selected passages from every section of the Bible to demonstrate the pervasive influence and ongoing relevance of honor and shame. Accordingly, readers can use this book in several ways.

First, you could read the book straight through, from beginning to end. Another option is to divide up the readings so that you meditate on and apply one entry per day. For pastors and teachers, the book contains a wealth of insights and suggestions to assist you in proclaiming God's word. Of course, some people will want to come back to the book multiple times to compare selected entries with whatever passage of Scripture they might be studying. In any case, we certainly recommend that you read each entry with your Bible open so that you can compare the interpretations offered here with the biblical text and its context.

Finally, these reflections aim at being practical and written to affect our heads, hearts, and hands. They intend to challenge how we think, what we desire, and the ways we live. For this book to bear fruit in your life, spend time meditating on the "Parting Reflections" and "Parting Prayer" at the end of each entry. We pray that the following pages will encourage you to love (*and so honor*) the Lord with all your mind, with all your heart, and with all your strength.

What Are Honor and Shame?

A primary purpose of this book is to open hearts and minds to how Scripture speaks about using honor and shame. This requires that we accomplish another goal: familiarize readers with the concepts of honor and shame. So, let's define our terms.

What about **honor**? A simple yet robust definition is this: Honor is a person's right to respect.[1] People claim a right to respect when they possess qualities that are deemed praiseworthy. In this sense, honor is a measure of one's worth. Its opposite, shame, requires more explanation.

Shame is the fear, pain, or state of being devalued according to some standard of worth. For instance, shame includes the sense that one lacks worth or falls short of various social criteria. This definition accounts for several types of shame. Keep in mind that researchers and writers routinely talk about shame in different ways.

First and most basic, shame refers to a person's sensitivity to the opinion of others. Humans are wired for social connection. We are sensitive to the opinions of others, even if we disagree with those opinions. We are aware

---

1. Frank Henderson Stewart, *Honor* (Chicago, IL: University of Chicago Press, 1994), 30–37.

Figure 1

and displeased when rejected, isolated, or scorned. Without this sensitivity, we have no capacity to become moral agents. Shamelessness is the path to immoral living. Accordingly, such sensitivity is the basic starting point for experiencing other types of shame.

Second, there is psychological shame, which is the sense of shame with which most people are probably familiar. It is an internal experience; it is an intense feeling of unworthiness. However, psychological shame is only one kind of shame. Third, anthropologists speak of social shame, which refers to a person's social worth or social identity. Bullying a person or mistreating people is one way of publicly shaming them. Fourth, the Bible includes what Brad calls "sacred shame." This includes our identity or image in relation to God.

Scripture alludes to each type of shame, so we don't imply that one type of shame is more true or good or biblical. Honor and shame are inherently relational, so these categories merely speak of shame in relation to oneself, society, and the sacred.

In the Bible, various words and concepts convey honor or shame. For example, being poor, sick, naked, a slave or a foreigner often carry negative, socially shameful connotations within the ancient world of the Bible. *Disgrace, dishonor, scorn*, and *reproach* belong to this same family of shame-related words.

Likewise, being clean, an heir, a priest, and sitting at a king's right hand can all communicate the concept of honor. The word *glory* serves as a functional synonym for honor. In "giving God glory," we are not adding to his fundamental nature; instead, we are acknowledging his infinite worth.

A Few Key Ideas and Concepts

Across cultures, people use similar metaphors to communicate issues of honor and shame. These varied metaphors were present in first-century Mediterranean culture and can thus be found throughout Scripture. As mentioned above, a goal of this book is to highlight and uncover these aspects of Scripture so that our understanding of God may be enlarged. Therefore, we will briefly explain several terms that you'll see in these pages and their connection to honor and shame.

Name, Reputation, Status, or "Face": Throughout the world, people are concerned about their reputations. Different cultures use various terms to explain this social phenomenon. Regardless, being concerned for one's name, reputation, status, or "face" has to do with achieving and maintaining both honor and harmony in relationships. In America, teenagers are particularly fascinated with their reputation. To maintain honor, they want to wear the right clothes or listen to the right music.

On the other hand, shame is the result when one's name is defamed. For instance, in Chinese culture, a person who "loses face" suffers some kind and degree of shame. To speak of a person's name, reputation, status, or "face" points to one's state of having honor or shame. This observation is not surprising since honor and shame are inherently social dynamics.

Collectivism/Group Membership: In general, Western cultures have an individualistic mindset. Individualist cultures tend to view each person as an autonomous individual largely responsible for their own fortunes. The interests of the individual are prioritized. Broadly speaking, these societies hold each person to similar standards for right and wrong, and every individual is supposed to follow them.

However, many cultures throughout the world, including ancient biblical cultures, lay greater stress on group membership. Such cultures are often described as "collectivistic." Instead of seeing individuals as being independent of one another, they are viewed as being *inter*dependent. Such cultures place significant value on harmony for the whole group and discourage instances where one person stands out above everyone else. Thus, the community expects each person to conform to predetermined social rules. To go along with the group and contribute to social harmony is honorable. To contradict these social norms is dishonorable and can result in exclusion and shame.

Status Reversal: This concept is present throughout Scripture. For example, through Christ's reconciling work on the cross, we who once were "alienated, hostile in mind, and doing evil deeds" are now presented as "holy and blameless, and above reproach" (Col. 1:21–22 ESV). We are called "out of darkness and into his marvelous light" (1 Pet. 2:9). Some think these texts primarily refer to the forgiveness of sin.

While this is a glorious truth, there is often more going on in Scripture than just a reversal from guilt to innocence. Throughout Scripture, we read about one's status being reversed from a position of shame to one of honor (e.g., Joseph in Egypt, Hannah, Jesus's mother Mary). God does not merely make us righteous through Christ, he also gives us great honor (John 17:22; Rom. 8:30).

Hospitality: In many cultures, hospitality is supremely important. This value is present in the Bible from the book of Genesis onward. Recall Abraham and Sarah's strong concern for hospitality in Genesis 18:1–15. Jesus also had much to say about hospitality (Luke 7:44–46). Across the world, showing great hospitality to a guest is to give them honor. To not show hospitality both dishonors the guest and is shameful for the host.

Reciprocity: To varying degrees, reciprocity is fundamental to all societies. Broadly, reciprocity refers to the exchange of favors and gifts for the sake of creating and sustaining relationships. Such practices are especially critical in collectivist communities. Not reciprocating favors would break from social expectations and be deemed shameful.

Comparison, Pride, People-Pleasing, Boasting: These terms are relatively similar and involve a concern for one's own honor. We boast or seek to please others because we want people to think highly of us. We compare ourselves to others because we are innately concerned with how we measure up. While seeking honor is not inherently sinful, how we seek it matters. Excessive pride ultimately results in shame: "Whoever exalts himself will be humbled, and whoever humbles himself will be exalted" (Matt. 3:12 ESV).

The following entries focus on the scriptural presence of honor, shame, and the various related terms just described. We want these brief devotions to encourage meditation on the gospel by digging into the quarry of biblical texts that use honor and shame. We hope that as you read them, new categories will open up in your mind and that the result will be a deeper love for God. Charles Spurgeon once said:

> The readiest way to be spiritually rich in heavenly knowledge is to dig in this mine of diamonds, to gather pearls from this heavenly sea. When Jesus sought to enrich others, he wrought in the quarry of Holy Scripture.[2]

The introduction will likely stimulate as many questions as answers. Still, we hope that it provides a framework for reading the following devotionals. As you move along in the book, feel free to refer back to these pages. May God bless you as you meditate on his word!

---

2. From the January 18 evening entry in C. H. Spurgeon, *Morning and Evening* (Wheaton, IL: Crossway, 2003).

OLD

TESTAMENT

The Genesis of Glory

—⫿⫿⫿⫿⫿—

Bless the Lord, O my soul! O Lord my God, you are very great! You are clothed with splendor and majesty, covering yourself with light as with a garment, stretching out the heavens like a tent.

—PS. 104:1–2 ESV

Each day, a vivid palette of color smears the Arizona morning and evening sky. Weary hikers trek nearby mountains, never tiring of the majestic sights. In these moments, when light and darkness separate day from night, we are gripped by the glory of God. While we lose our breath in awe, the Bible reminds us that God merely spoke and brought the earth into existence. Among ancient creation stories, this manner of making the world is unique to the Lord. This explains the opening words of Psalm 104, an explicit meditation on Genesis 1.

"The heavens are telling the glory of God; and the firmament proclaims his handiwork" (Ps. 19:1). The Creator establishes order and bestows beauty. The Lord creates the world to be the place where He dwells with his people. Even as the Bible depicts the Garden of Eden as a sacred space, it is like a temple. Creation forever invites us into worship. Light, land, and water perfectly function together to sustain life. Therefore, the psalmist exclaims, "O Lord, how manifold are your works! In wisdom have you made them all; the earth is full of your creatures" (Ps. 104:24).

Before God spoke, the earth was a formless void, and such are we, apart from the Lord's creative work. So why does he make a people for himself? For the sake of his glory (Isa. 43:7). Creation gives witness to God's sovereign generosity (Acts 14:17). In Athens, Paul highlights an implication of the creation story. The Lord is worthy of fame; false idols are a façade. The Creator God "does not live in temples made by man, nor is he served by human hands, as though he needed anything, since he himself gives to all mankind life and breath and everything" (Acts 17:24–25 ESV).

We are sometimes prone to boast about our efforts and successes. We climb mountains and make a name for ourselves. But we forget the one who creates the earth below and the sky above, without which we would not have light, water, or food. Like Job, let us be silent before God. And then, when we're ready to speak, we will sing, "O Lord, our Lord, how majestic is your name in all the earth! You have set your glory above the heavens" (Ps. 8:1 ESV).

Parting Reflection

We mirror God's creativity in countless ways, though none match his work in creating the world. What is something that makes you marvel with awe? Why does it make you marvel? Spend time today or this week reflecting on the beauty of God's handiwork.

Parting Prayer

We confess that our minds have put boundaries around our imaginations, unable to conceive of your awesome power and wisdom. Father, you care for the smallest details of our lives with the same attention that you design the veins that feed a leaf. We delight in you and long to make your name known among all nations.

Crowned with Honor

———— ⑾ ————

Then God said, "Let us make humankind in our image, according to our likeness; and let them have dominion over the fish of the sea, and over the birds of the air, and over the cattle, and over all the wild animals of the earth, and over every creeping thing that creeps upon the earth." So God created humankind in his image, in the image of God he created them; male and female he created them.

—GEN. 1:26–27

Growing up, our East Texan, working-class family, didn't have much money. My mother even called herself "trailer trash," a reference to our living in cheap mobile homes. When we finally moved into a house, she celebrated like the heaven itself had opened up. Still, we lived in a poor neighborhood. And our second-hand clothing meant we carried our shame on our backs. As a result, I felt isolated from others, like I didn't belong.

This is not God's intention for life. Instead, Genesis 1–2 displays a fundamental harmony between people. God formed humanity, male and female, in his likeness. Within Eden's Garden temple, Adam and Eve are images of the Creator God.[3] Along with them, our vocation is to "be fruitful and multiply and fill the earth and subdue it, and have dominion over the fish of the sea and over the birds of the heavens and over every living thing that moves on the earth" (Gen. 1:28 ESV). For this reason, Genesis 1:31 says, "And God saw everything that he had made, and behold, it was very good" (ESV). Sadly, this memory fades from our minds when we see images of death and injustice everywhere we turn. No wonder many Christians emphasize the pervasive power of sin. Modern hymns profess that there is nothing good in us, while theologians speak of "original sin" and our separation from God.

---

3. See the previous entry "The Genesis of Glory."

But what about humanity's original glory? Psalm 8 calls us to meditate on this point, "You have made them a little lower than God, and *crowned them with glory and honor.* You have given them dominion over the works of your hands; you have put all things under their feet" (Ps. 8:5–6, emphasis added). Ancient kings erected images of themselves throughout their dominion. These lifeless statues project a king's majesty. However, Genesis says humans serve as *living* reflections of the glory of God. As we carefully tend to God's sacred creation, we demonstrate that all creation is all for him.

Our original glory consists of our vocation as God's image-bearers. We belong to him. No wonder "the man and his wife were both naked, and were not ashamed" (Gen. 2:25). The Creator has blessed us with a capacity for great fruitfulness. We are not costume jewelry, superficially beautiful but essentially worthless. Instead, we are like tarnished silver, having priceless value, imbued with majestic glory. Regardless of how humble your beginnings were, know that from creation you have been crowned with honor.

Parting Reflection

Do you tend to dwell too much on your perceived lack of worth, inability to measure up to people's expectations, or other shortcomings? How would truly understanding and embracing this glory and honor that God gives change how you live?

Parting Prayer

Like the psalmist in Psalm 8:1, 3–4, we also pray:

> *O Lord, our Sovereign, how majestic is your name in all the earth! When I look at your heavens, the work of your fingers, the moon, and the stars that you have established; what are human beings that you are mindful of them, mortals that you care for them?*

Thank you that you grant us the privilege of reflecting your honor. Holy Spirit, continue to remove the tarnish so that we may shine for your glory as we continually grow in our allegiance to you.

The Nature of Shame

And the man and his wife were both naked, and were not ashamed.

—GEN. 2:25

Yes, I sinned, but it wasn't the sense of guilt that nearly killed me. It was shame. In high school, I compromised spiritually. My public reputation meant I couldn't let people know about my moral failures. But my conscience knew even what I hid from others. In one year, shame almost ended my life twice.

Shame is the fear, pain, or state of being regarded as lacking value or worth.[4] Reasons for shame vary. Some are moral; others are not. Shame warps our sense of identity. Scientists find that our brains react to shame as though it is a physical threat. Our brains can't distinguish between the two. The consequences are devastating and long-lasting.

Genesis 3 illustrates shame's impact. The man and woman are without shame in Genesis 2:25, but everything soon changes. After eating the forbidden fruit, we see three characteristic responses to shame. First, the couple covers and hides themselves (3:7–8). Shame makes us feel vulnerable and compels us to withdraw. Second, shame evokes fear (3:10). The man and woman fear exposure and the eventual consequences. They attempt to protect themselves. Third, people experiencing shame shift blame (3:12–13). This defense strategy deflects negative attention. At the same time, it shatters relationships.

The Lord then says, "You are dust, and to dust you shall return" (3:19). Despite their humble state, God honors them. God singles out one forbidden tree and tells them not to eat from it. And yet, they do. Now they find themselves isolated, exiled from home (3:23–24). Like this couple, we try to find fig leaves to cover our shame. These come in many forms, like Facebook and

---

4. See the Introduction for an expanded explanation of terms.

Instagram where we often present our lives as picturesque. Unsurprisingly, social media breeds much shame and isolation as we are constantly comparing ourselves to others.

Thankfully, the Lord does not leave Adam and Eve or us to wallow in shame. "And the Lord God made garments of skins for the man and for his wife, and clothed them" (3:21). They are his. They bear his image. One day, the woman's seed will crush evil under his feet, putting the tempting serpent to shame, while restoring us to a position of honor.

For this reason, Paul clearly draws from Genesis when he speaks of Christ and our hope. Comparing our body to a tent, he says in 2 Corinthians 5:2–4 ESV (cf. 1 Cor. 15:53):

> For in this tent we groan, longing to put on our heavenly dwelling, if indeed by putting it on we may not be found naked. For while we are still in this tent, we groan, being burdened—not that we would be unclothed, but that we would be further clothed, so that what is mortal may be swallowed up by life.

Parting Reflection

Shame typically affects us in more pervasive and destructive ways than do feelings of guilt. How have you reacted to experiences of shame? How have you responded to shame in ways similar to what we see in Genesis 3?

Parting Prayer

Father, you did not create us to wallow in shame. Thank you for a gospel that forms a new community, the church, among whom we can be honest about our shame. We praise you Jesus for enduring utter isolation upon the cross so that we might be covered with righteousness.

Competing for Attention

———————— ⑉ ————————

And the Lord had regard for Abel and his offering, but for Cain and his offering he had no regard. So Cain was very angry, and his countenance fell.

—GEN. 4:4–5 ESV

The entire staff wished me a happy birthday, yet my smile hid my anxiety. After all, I was 23 years old and hadn't planted a church. My mentor planted his first church at my age. I worried about the kind of "failure" I'd become if I didn't hurry up. My college pastor liked to say, "Comparison is the thief of joy." Apparently, I didn't listen. Before long, I learned how right he was. My ambition to match his achievement led to frustration, burnout, and bitterness.

We all compete for the attention of others. Sometimes, it's the praise of parents or the admiration of friends. Although Cain sought God's approval, he did so in an utterly misguided way. Cain, a tiller of the ground, gave an offering of fruit to the Lord. His younger brother, Abel, kept sheep and brought fat portions from the first of his flock. Because the Lord had regard for Abel's offering, Cain grew jealous. Comparison and competition gave birth to the root of bitterness. His anger then drove him to kill his brother.

Why? Cain desired "face" too much.

"Then the Lord said to Cain, 'Where is Abel your brother?' He said, 'I do not know; am I my brother's keeper'" (Gen. 4:9 ESV)? Notice Cain's implicit criticism. He doesn't want to be responsible for other people. He refuses to submit to anyone else. If Cain cannot have God's praise, then he demands his independence. Cain wants a relationship with God but with an implicit condition: Cain wants God to honor him blindly, irrespective of character.

Though a farmer, Cain didn't understand the roots of his discontent. His sense of worth depended on outperforming someone else. He didn't truly seek God's approval. Furthermore, Abel had become a potential tool for Cain to exalt himself. In effect, Cain would have a relationship with others, including the Lord, only if they were willing to recognize and praise his importance, thus giving him "face." Competing for attention and constant comparison leads to frustration, burnout, and bitterness. Instead, we must learn to seek the honor that comes from God alone.

Parting Reflection

Sadly, we constantly measure our worth by comparing ourselves to others. When have you been upset or bothered that someone else received the recognition that you felt you deserved? Beyond mere pride, what specifically caused this reaction in your heart?

Parting Prayer

Father, you have accepted us because of Christ. Yet, we confess that we have been jealous of others. We have sought the approval of other people above the praise that comes from you. We praise you for your patience and grace. In our lives, exalt your name above our own!

Two Sources of Honor

———————— ⑾ ————————

Then they said, "Come, let us build ourselves a city, and a tower with its top in the heavens, and let us make a name for ourselves; otherwise we shall be scattered abroad upon the face of the whole earth."

—GEN. 11:4

The desire for recognition is the primary engine that drives human history.[5] This observation captures a key insight from Genesis 11–12. In all our relationships, we want honor and recognition. And this is OK! God has wired us this way (Rom. 2:7, 10, 29). What matters most is the source of and reason for which we seek recognition.

What motivates the people who build the tower at Babel? They seek to "make a name" for themselves. Why? They're afraid and don't want to be scattered. They are fostering a reputation and projecting unity become defense mechanisms, birthed from a prideful attitude. How does the Lord humble them? He says, "Come, let us go down, and confuse their language there, so that they will not understand one another's speech" (Gen. 11:7). Pride creates factions and destroys families. We begin to use relationships for mere personal benefit, often settling for recognition that is superficial and transient. For those who build the tower at Babel, their efforts to receive honor and recognition crumble because they seek them apart from and outside of God's will (Gen. 1:28; 9:1).

Genesis 12 directly contrasts the Babel story. God takes the initiative to develop a relationship with Abram (whose name is later changed to Abraham). The Lord says, "Go from your country and your kindred and your father's house to the land that I will show you" (Gen. 12:1). No doubt this command could have caused the same kind of fear felt by the people at Babel. But

---

5. Francis Fukuyama, *The End of History* (London: Penguin, 2012).

Abraham responds not with dread but with a faith that glorifies God (Rom. 4:20). While those at Babel seek to make a name for themselves, God keeps his promise to make a name for Abraham (Gen. 12:2). Abraham allows himself to be scattered through faith in God. What results from Abraham's obedience? The Lord brings humanity together. He promises, "in you all the families of the earth shall be blessed" (Gen. 12:3).

These stories illustrate two sources of honor. The first is self-serving and outside of God's will. The other comes through faith in and obedience to God, the true source of lasting honor. Similarly, many people today try to make a name for themselves based on titles, accomplishments, education, and even cultural identity. Yet, the Lord gives honor that endures.

Parting Reflection

In what areas of life do you seek recognition or honor? Perhaps education, clothing, or how you present yourself on social media? Since desiring honor isn't wrong in and of itself, what would it look like to bring these areas of your life under God's authority?

Parting Prayer

Lord, we thank you that we can read and learn from your word. We confess that we often seek honor and recognition for ourselves alone. Lord, help us to be more like Abraham by obeying you, trusting that only the honor that comes from you truly matters.

Treating People Like Objects

———————— ⬦ ————————

Then Leah said, "God has endowed me with a good dowry; now my husband will honor me, because I have borne him six sons"; so she named him Zebulun.

—GEN. 30:20

Imagine being sold to a man by your father. For Leah and Rachel, this was their reality. Two daughters in exchange for 14 years of labor (Gen. 29:27). Marriage offered them little change. Their husband, Jacob, preferred Rachel because he judged her more beautiful than Leah (Gen. 29:17). Because Jacob disregarded Leah, the Lord enabled her to bear many children while Rachel remained barren. These women endured a lifetime of being objectified and treated as commodities for trade. The men around them viewed their bodies as things to be used for personal gain, whether financial profit, lustful pleasure or giving birth.

Far from honoring these women as valuable, such treatment breeds shame. Their worth seemingly depended on whether they were "enough" in the eyes of the judging other. Whatever praise they might receive was superficial and fleeting. Despite Leah's fertility, her shame was acute. Again and again, she hoped that the next birth would finally secure Jacob's affection (Gen. 29:32, 34; 30:20).

These attitudes and actions foster competition more than compassion. A cycle of shame and rivalry drives these sisters to engage in the same sinful behavior that entrapped them, as when Leah sells mandrakes to Rachel so that Leah can sleep with Jacob (Gen. 30:14–16). These problems fester into generational plagues. Years later, Rachel and Leah's children are consumed with jealousy and sell Joseph into slavery.

David Zahl says, "Our religion is that which we rely on not just for meaning or hope but *enoughness* . . . We believe instinctively that, were we to reach some benchmark in our minds, then value, vindication, and love would be ours—that if we got enough, we would *be* enough."[6] The truth is sobering. We are not God. We can never have everything nor be everything. And so, we compensate by comparing ourselves. We start to view others or ourselves as objects, not people made in God's image. Questions consume our minds, like "Do I measure up? Do they?" Our zeal for counterfeit honor only opens a door for shame.

Parting Reflection

How might we treat others in ways that communicate that we value them only because of the benefits they bring us? How have you felt shame when people act this way toward you?

Parting Prayer

Father, you do not accept us because we are "enough" by worldly standards. We have value because you delight in us. Your love is enough even when we fall short. Help us not to shame others. Spirit, open our eyes to see other people as worthy of honor and love.

---

6. David Zahl, *Seculosity* (Minneapolis, MN: Fortress Press, 2019), 11. Italics in the original.

Why Does God Send the Plagues?

———— ·⫴|⫴· ————

I will send all my plagues upon you yourself, and upon your officials,
and upon your people, so that you may know that there is no one like
me in all the earth.

—EXOD. 9:14

For centuries, ancient Israel suffered under the enslaving whip of Egypt. And right when God promises to redeem them, he seemingly takes his time, sending ten plagues rather than rescuing them all at once. Why doesn't he end this unjust oppression right away? From the beginning, the Lord clearly states his intention to Moses:

> *When Pharaoh does not listen to you, I will lay my hand upon Egypt and bring*
> *my people the Israelites, company by company, out of the land of Egypt by great*
> *acts of judgment.* The Egyptians shall know that I am the Lord, *when I stretch*
> *out my hand against Egypt and bring the Israelites out from among them.*
> —Exod. 7:4–5 (emphasis added).[7]

The Lord not only wants to eradicate social evils but also seeks to make a name for himself. He desires that the world may delight in the one true Creator God. He is worthy of being loved and lauded. The plagues manifest the Lord's patience and power as he prods human hearts to repent and worship. During Passover, Israel celebrates God's mercy amid the climactic final plague. The sacrificed Passover lamb is God's means of judging Pharoah and

---

7. See Exodus 6:7; 7:17; 8:10, 22–23; 9:14–16. Cf. 1 Chronicles 17:21; Jeremiah 32:30; Ezekiel 20:9–10; Daniel 9:15.

the Egyptian gods.[8] This victory ensures that the surrounding nations will know of the Lord's great deliverance, and so honor him.

Israel was quite aware of God's purposes. On multiple occasions, Moses intercedes with the Lord on Israel's behalf. The nation openly rebels, first by worshipping a golden calf and later by complaining against his leadership. When the Lord threatens to punish the people, how does Moses respond? He states that rejecting his people would stain the Lord's holy reputation as the faithful and sovereign God.[9]

Similarly, God not only cares about what we do but also *how* we do it. We who bear his name are invited to seek glory and honor but notice how: "by patiently doing good" (Rom. 2:7). Whether magnificent or mundane, we are called to do everything for the glory of God (1 Cor. 10:31).

Parting Reflection

God shows wisdom in all he does, including *how* he accomplishes his purposes. Think of a time when you did not understand God's ways. How might he have wanted to reveal himself to you in a particular way during that time?

Parting Prayer

Father, nothing is more loving than that you reveal yourself to us so that we might know and love you. Your wisdom, power, and mercy are so evident in Christ. Soften our hearts when we are unteachable so that we may delight in you.

---

8. Exodus 12:12; Numbers 33:4.
9. Exodus 32:12; Numbers 14:13–16; Deuteronomy 9:27–29; 29:24–25.

Bearing God's Name

——————— ⫴ ———————

You shall not take the name of the Lord your God in vain, for the Lord will not hold him guiltless who takes his name in vain.

—EXOD. 20:7 ESV

In middle and high school, one's brand of apparel or shoes is a marker of status. I always felt second-class because my parents couldn't afford to buy me Z Cavaricci pants or Air Jordan shoes. Marketers are geniuses in making us *want* to advertise *for them*. Think about it—people think it's "cool" to display the Nike swoosh or other brand logos. Meanwhile, those companies benefit from the advertising that *we* pay *them* to provide.

These dynamics shed light on an often misunderstand commandment. Many people learn the Ten Commandments as children growing up in church. They're often taught that we shouldn't use the Lord's name to swear or in any improper way. While we're familiar with this third commandment, we don't always grasp its deeper significance.

As scholars observe, the central concern of the commandment is "wearing the name of Yahweh as a badge or a brand of ownership."[10] With that said, we certainly don't want to speak in ways that dishonor the Lord. However, the command implies much more. As God's people, we bear or "carry" his name wherever we go. We represent him in the world in a similar way that international travelers sew their nation's flag on their backpacks. The way we live reflects on the character of our God, whether for honor or dishonor.

As followers of Christ, it's as if we are branded with his name upon us. We cannot remove it, though we sometimes think we can discard his name from us when we go to work or hang out with friends. Paul uses a similar analogy,

---

10. Daniel Block, "Bearing the Name of the Lord with Honor." *Bibliotheca Sacra* 168 no. 22 (January–March 2011): 20–31.

"For as many of you as were baptized into Christ have put on Christ" (Gal. 3:27 ESV). If we live as though we could take off Christ, as if he were merely a fashionable garment, we take the name of the Lord our God in vain. Bearing God's name means that we belong to him, not he to us. And just as one cannot casually remove a branding or tattoo, so we are called to honor the Lord in every sphere of life. Wherever we go, his name goes with us.

Parting Reflection

How does your life "advertise" for the Lord? Do you get as excited about bearing the Lord's name as you do certain brands of shoes, clothing, technology, or other items?

Parting Prayer

Father, we belong to you. We bear your name, and you go wherever your name goes. We rejoice in that! Forgive us when we foster our personal reputation and "brand" yet overlook how we represent you in the world. Help us to be worthy ambassadors of Christ.

Honor Your Father and Mother

———————— ⑈⑈⑈ ————————

Honor your father and your mother, so that your days may be long in the land that the Lord your God is giving you.

—EXOD. 20:12

I have heard the Chinese say it time and again: "Americans don't honor their parents." "Why do you say that?" I'd ask. They always replied, "Because you put them in nursing homes." A few things explain this common impression. First, nursing homes in China had a bad reputation, and many Chinese do not understand how nice American nursing homes can be. Second, my friends assumed that elderly parents should live with their children. Little did they realize that many American parents don't want to be a burden on their kids. Instead, they prefer the independence and friendship afforded them by living in a nursing home.

Culture affects how we see the parent-child relationship. In contrast to most Chinese, American adults see themselves as independent from their parents. What happens then when they read Exodus 20:12? Western Christians often assume it primarily speaks to young children still living in the home. Given the historical and biblical context, this is not likely.[11] Instead, it addresses adult children, like other commandments such as, "you shall not covet your neighbor's wife" (Exod. 20:17).

The fifth command gets practical quickly. For example, aging parents increasingly have health issues. They may have financial needs. For Jesus, providing such support for parents is a sacred responsibility (Matt. 15:3–6; Mark 7:11–13). Paul even stresses, "And whoever does not provide for relatives, and especially for family members, has denied the faith and is worse than an

---

11. Charlie Trimm, "Honor Your Parents: A Command for Adults." *JETS* 60, no. 2 (June 2017): 247–63.

unbeliever" (1 Tim. 5:8). The writer of Proverbs 23:22 warns, "do not despise your mother *when she is old*" (emphasis added). Likewise, "Those who do violence to their father and chase away their mother are children who cause shame and bring reproach" (Prov. 19:26).

Honoring one's parents doesn't require absolute obedience, particularly when they lead children to sin (Ezek. 20:18). It does entail a proper attitude, one that acknowledges parents' worth. The Hebrew word for honor conveys the idea of "weight" or "heaviness." And so, we recognize the calling God gives to parents, even though all fall short. Charlie Trimm states, "while parents are human, how children treat them is often indicative of how they treat God. This is the kind of son who will not take care of his parents."[12]

Parting Application

Take some time to reach out to your mother, father, or other parental figures. Express appreciation for the way that God has used them to bless you. Inquire how you might bless them in some practical way.

Parting Prayer

You are our heavenly Father, the God who gave us birth. Our days are entirely in your hands. Forgive us for the ways we have dishonored those elders in our lives who have raised us and protected our way. May we learn to honor you better as we grow in humility as adult children.

---

12. Trimm, 254.

Sanctified as Worthy of Unique Honor

———————— ·⫴⫴⫴·· ————————

Then Moses said to Aaron, "This is what the Lord has said: 'Among those who are near me I will be sanctified, and before all the people I will be glorified.'" And Aaron held his peace.

—LEV. 10:3

Why does Leviticus focus so much on the sacrifices? From start to end, the book is all about holiness. Though often viewed as a religious word, the meaning of holiness is easily grasped when seen through the lens of honor. To call things or people holy is to set them apart as worthy of unique honor. In effect, people reckon as holy whatever they judge to have supreme value. We worship God as holy because he is uniquely worthy of praise and adoration. But what about land, the tabernacle, instruments of worship, and even certain people in the Bible? They are considered holy because of their special relationship with God. Their holiness is derived from God's divine honor. Furthermore, God's people reflect God's honor by living holy lives (i.e., living a life worthy of honor).

This insight sheds light on several passages concerning the use of sacrifices. God kills Aaron's sons, Nadab and Abihu, for offering "unholy fire before the Lord" (Lev. 10:1). Leviticus 10:3 tells us why: "Among those who are near me I will be sanctified, and before all the people I will be glorified" (ESV). God's being sanctified (or "shown holy") is explained by his being glorified. Verse 10 of Leviticus 10 clarifies a fundamental aspect of glorifying God: "You are to distinguish between the holy and the common, and between the unclean and the clean" (ESV). Put simply, Aaron's sons did not treat the Lord as worthy of unique honor. God's response is not so much about setting an example as it is about expressing the reality that God will not be mocked.

A primary purpose of sacrifice in Scripture is to sanctify or honor God. This results in atonement (Lev. 10:17; cf. Lev. 9:6–7). Reconciliation and ongoing relationship with God necessitate that we see God's unsurpassed glory. Therefore, our hearts set him apart as holy. When the Lord grants us his Holy Spirit, he manifests his unique glory in our lives. We are sanctified by his glory (Exod. 29:43–44). In so doing, the sacrificial system not only brings honor to God; it also removes our shame as we reflect his glorious character.

Parting Reflection

How have you previously understood the purposes of sacrifices? How has honor or shame influenced your perspective? What might it mean for us to "present your bodies as a living sacrifice, holy and acceptable to God" (Rom. 12:1)?

Parting Prayer

Lord, we often treat other things as holy, deserving of unique honor. This is idolatry. We confess that you alone are worthy of most lavish praise. Our honor stems from our relationship with you, for you have set us apart for your special purposes.

May God's Face Shine Upon Us

———————— ⑈ ————————

The Lord bless you and keep you; the Lord make his face to shine upon you, and be gracious to you; the Lord lift up his countenance upon you, and give you peace.

—NUM. 6:24–26

You have likely had this blessing read over you at the end of a church service at some point. If you're like me, the part about God blessing and keeping us seems comprehensible enough. At the same time, the words about God making "his face to shine upon [us]" and lifting "up his countenance upon [us]" have always felt a bit puzzling. However, these words were not confusing to the original audience, nor are they to many Christians throughout the world today. These cultural expressions concern honor and shame. Specifically, they involve the concept of "face," an idea prevalent in many traditional cultures throughout the world.

Some scholars say that "face" is an "intoxicating metaphor that connects communication with social life."[13] Another offers a more comprehensible explanation: "A concern for face . . . is indicative of other directedness, that is, having sensitivity to how one appears in the eyes of others and a tendency to act in ways which meet their approval."[14] These explanations shed light on Psalm 34:5: "Those who look to him are radiant, and their face shall never be ashamed" (ESV). The psalmist calls us to look to God and to be aware

---

13. Stella Ting-Toomey and Beth-Ann Cocroft, "Face and Facework: Theoretical and Research Issues," in *The Challenge of Facework: Cross-Cultural and Interpersonal Issues* (Albany, NY: State University of New York Press, 1994), 307.

14. David Yau-fai Ho, "On the Concept of Face," *American Journal of Sociology* 81, no. 4 (1976): 867.

of how we appear before him. In doing so, we orient our lives in a way that pleases him.

Returning to Numbers 6, how are we to understand this prayer of blessing in light of Christ? It is God's promise to his people that when we come to him through Jesus, we will be blessed with his presence. Werner Mischke says, "The 'face' of God's people—that is, their honor—is inextricably linked to the experience of beholding the face of God. It is assumed that intimacy with God is possible, intimacy as close as face to face."[15] And so, this benediction draws us into intimacy with God. It also beckons us to orient our lives in a way that pleases him. Neither blessing is ultimately accomplished except by Christ.

Parting Reflection

Are you sensitive to how you appear in God's eyes? Do you tend to act in ways that seek his approval? How has Jesus ensured that God's face will in fact shine upon us? Why is this important and how does it impact the way that we live?

Parting Prayer

Father, thank you that your promises are true. We want to have a radiant and joy-filled life that flows from experiencing your presence. Aside from just knowing true things about you, help us to order our lives in such a way that we look to you with confidence, knowing that you want to bless us. May we seek your face, O Lord. Make your face to shine upon us today.

---

15. Werner Mischke, *The Global Gospel: Achieving Missional Impact in Our Multicultural World* (Scottsdale, AZ: Mission ONE, 2015), 114.

A Covenant Mediator

———————— ⢀⣿⡀ ————————

How long will this people despise me? And how long will they refuse to believe in me, in spite of all the signs that I have done among them? I will strike them with pestilence and disinherit them, and I will make of you a nation greater and mightier than they.

—NUM. 14:11–12

Westerners often read a passage like this and think, "Why in the world would God say this?" Or perhaps we explain it away: "Maybe God is just testing Moses to see how he will respond." There's probably an element of truth to the latter, but it's not a wholly satisfying explanation. We know that Moses replies by reminding God that if he does wipe out the Israelites, word will get back to the Egyptians. God's name will be slandered. He will appear weak or unfaithful, as though he brought them out of Egypt only to kill them. This was not new information to God, and he didn't need Moses's reminder as though God would say, "Oh yeah, you're right, good point!" and then change his mind. God was never going to fully disinherit the Israelites (although he rightfully could have). So, what's going on here in this passage?

A typical explanation for Numbers 14 is that it serves to highlight the need for a covenant mediator between God and humanity. The central purpose of a mediator is to "secure peace between two warring parties."[16] Additionally, the role of a mediator is not merely legal; it's deeply relational. A mediator seeks to preserve the relationship that existed before the conflict. In our case, if we're honest, we know that we're in constant need of a mediator. We need a go-between that gives us access to God so that we may live how we were created to. In traditional honor-shame cultures, mediators play a far more

---

16. R. C. Sproul, "The One Mediator," https://www.ligonier.org/learn/devotionals/the-one-mediator/.

significant role than many Westerners might expect. In those cultures, law courts are weak compared to the power of relational bonds. Mediators must be people of honor, and they must show fidelity. The opposing parties might not trust each other, but out of respect for the mediator, because they give him "face," they're willing to consider reconciliation.

The Old Testament foreshadows the need for an ultimate mediator. Moses regularly plays this role for the Israelites: in the fallout from the Golden Calf (Exod. 32:11–14), when a fire burned through Israel's camp (Num. 11:1–2), and with the bronze serpent (Num. 21:4–9). After Moses, the priests served as mediators for Israel. However, these human mediators were insufficient, constantly replaced by others (Heb. 8:23). Today, we know these mediators point to Jesus, the one true mediator between God and man (1 Tim. 2:5). He is the faithful and honorable one. Jesus gives us boldness to enter God's presence with prayer.

Parting Reflection

Jesus's role as mediator is not simply legal. It is deeply relational. How might the relational character of Jesus appeal to someone from a predominately honor-shame culture?

Parting Prayer

Lord, we praise you for all the beautiful aspects of salvation. We know that being God himself, Jesus is the only one who can rightly approach the Father. And as a human, Jesus is rightly fit to represent us before the Father. In light of these truths, we say, "In Jesus's name, Amen."

The Threat of Disinheritance

———————— ⫶⎹⎹⎸⫶ ————————

How long will this people despise me? And how long will they not believe in me, in spite of all the signs that I have done among them? I will strike them with the pestilence and disinherit them, and I will make of you a nation greater and mightier than they.

—NUM. 14:11–12

This passage offers a lot to chew on. Highlighting our need for a mediator is one takeaway. However, there is more to glean, specifically concerning God's threat to disinherit Israel. After all, Paul says that God's judgment on the Israelites in the Old Testament "occurred as examples for us, so that we might not desire evil as they did" (1 Cor. 10:6). Perhaps an aspect of Chinese culture can reveal another layer of meaning in Numbers 14.

In Chinese culture, by the age of just two-and-a-half, children are already socialized to be sensitive to shame. Chinese parents often use shaming techniques to ensure their child's compliance. For example, if a child has done something that dishonors the family, parents might suggest that family members go on an outing together but at the same time, hint at leaving the child at home. This action is intended to induce shame in the child. The ultimate goal of this shaming is not to bring shame in and of itself. Instead, it is in part to help the child to understand and fulfill their societal responsibilities.[17] One article encapsulates the point: "In Chinese culture, if a person is perceived as having no sense of shame, that person may be thought of as beyond moral reach and therefore is even 'feared by the devil.' Thus, shame to the Chinese is

---

17. Heidi Fung, "Becoming a Moral Child: The Socialization of Shame among Young Chinese Children." *American Anthropological Association. Ethos* 27, no. 2 (June 1999): 180–209.

not a mere emotion but also a moral and virtuous sensibility to be pursued."[18] Accordingly, honoring one's parents and not bringing shame on them is directly related to fulfilling one's societal responsibilities and thus morality.

To Westerners, the threat of disinheritance in Numbers 14 may not stand out. But in honor-shame cultures, the concept of inheritance goes far beyond receiving money or property after the death of one's parents. It has a much more comprehensive meaning. And so, when we read, "I will strike them with the pestilence and disinherit them," we are meant to feel the weight of the shame that comes along with disinheritance. As Paul reminds us, this passage serves as an example for us to not desire evil as the Israelites did. Instead, we should contemplate how dishonoring God brings shame upon ourselves and others. We are meant to further grasp the importance of upholding our societal responsibilities among God's people. We are beckoned to feel a sense of shame over our sins and repent of them.

Parting Reflection

Reread Numbers 14:11. How have you been like the Israelites, despising God and not believing in him despite all the signs that he has done among you?

Parting Prayer

Lord, thank you for giving us your word and these stories as examples to us. Help us to learn from those who went before us and not to desire evil as some did.

---

18. Jin Li, Lianquin Wang, and Kurt Fischer, "The Organization of Chinese Shame Concepts?" *Cognition & Emotion* 18, no. 6 (October 2004): 767–797.

Balaam's Shameless Quest for Honor

──────── ·⑾· ────────

Although Balak were to give me his house full of silver and gold, I could not go beyond the command of the Lord my God, to do less or more. You remain here, as the others did, so that I may learn what more the Lord may say to me.

—NUM. 22:18–19

The entertaining story of Numbers 22–24 is confusing on its face. After the Israelites defeat the Amorite kings, they move into the plains of Moab. Word of their escape from Egypt and recent victories spreads throughout the region. Understandably, the king of the Moab, Balak, is greatly concerned and fears the Israelites. So, he summons a pagan prophet named Balaam to curse Israel. God appears to permit Balaam to go with Balak's men but then gets angry when he actually goes. After the Lord halts him on the way via his donkey, Balaam says he will turn back but God again allows him to go so long as he speaks as directed. All in all, Balaam is slightly misguided but ultimately does the honorable thing, right? Not quite.

Balaam puts on a principled front, saying that he can't be bought and won't go beyond God's word. However, his actions suggest otherwise. When first summoned, he refuses to go with Balak's messengers after God plainly prohibits him (Num. 22:12). Balak then immediately sends more honorable princes and extra money to get Balaam's attention. This suggests that Balak's first group got the impression that Balaam could be bought at a price. They were right. After saying no a second time, Balaam adds, "You remain here, as the others did, so that I may learn what more the Lord may say to me" (Num. 22:19). Instead of firmly rejecting them, he holds the door open. He is enticed by the riches and honor that the king of Moab offers him and agrees to go. And although Balaam blesses Israel in multiple oracles, the rest of Scripture condemns his actions.

Immediately after Balaam's fourth oracle, the Israelites worship the false gods of the Moabites (Num. 25:1–3). Moses later tells us that Balaam advised the Moabites to entice the Israelites to "act treacherously against the Lord" (Num. 31:16). The early church similarly held a negative view of Balaam. Revelation 2:14 confirms Moses's words, and Peter declares Balaam to be a false teacher who "loved gain from wrongdoing" (2 Pet. 2:15 ESV).

Balaam had the distinct honor of the Lord speaking directly to him. And although he put on a principled front, his supposed integrity was a sham. He was shameless, preferring the honor and gain that this world has to offer over and against that which comes from God.

Parting Reflection

Do you know anyone who has put on a front of honoring the Lord, but only does so for earthly gain or respect? Have you? How can we guard against such a perilous error?

Parting Prayer

Lord, we confess that we have used your name for our own gain at various points. Thank you for your forgiveness. Protect us from the error of Balaam and help us to be content with the supreme honor that comes from being your child.

Honoring God with Our Theology

———————— ⫸⫷ ————————

You shall not make for yourself an idol, whether in the form of anything
that is in heaven above, or that is on the earth beneath, or that is in
the water under the earth. You shall not bow down to them or worship
them; for I the Lord your God am a jealous God.

—DEUT. 5:8–9

True godliness is not aimless or unanchored to a foundation. As John Calvin explained, it is "opposed to giddy license."[19] Thus, godliness in its truest sense stands on a firm foundation and "keeps itself within its proper limits."[20] This firm foundation is our theology. It consists of our knowledge of God and should be largely informed by the Scriptures through the work of the Spirit. In many respects, whether we honor God depends on our theology, as our thoughts inevitably inform our actions. To this end, Calvin said that the "knowledge of God does not rest in cold speculation but carries with it the honoring of him."[21] In other words, theology is not just for academics in ivory towers. Instead, theology anchors our faith and helps us to stay within the proper limits prescribed by God so as to properly honor and worship him. Let's consider idolatry as an example.

From reading Scripture or looking at the world around us, we see plenty of examples of humans worshiping idols. A prominent biblical example is the golden calf in Exodus 32, where God's people stepped outside the bounds of what can truly be called worship. While we may not make or worship a golden calf, there are certain areas of our lives that we too turn into idols. For

---

19. John Calvin, *The Institutes of the Christian Religion*, Volume 1, ed. John T. McNeill. (Louisville, KY: Westminster John Knox Press, 2006), 117.
20. Calvin, 117.
21. Calvin, 116.

example, we may idolize money, a certain relationship, or our family. And the Bible is not silent on these issues. If we don't have a proper theology, or worse yet, if we bury our heads in the sand and ignore a proper theology of various issues, we are prone to wander outside the limits that God has prescribed. Therefore, we will dishonor him with our actions.

God explains and defines what proper worship of him entails so that we will know how to serve him honorably. And praise be to God that there is not a rigid formula for how to worship. Instead, there are myriad ways that we can do so. That said, if we aren't anchored to the Bible and become wayward with worship, we are no longer truly honoring him. Thus, when we carefully consider our theology and seek to understand the Scriptures by the power of the Spirit, we are in a better position to truly honor and worship God.

Parting Reflection

In John 4:23, Jesus tells the woman of Samaria that "true worshippers will worship the Father in spirit and truth." We might also understand him as saying that we must worship God with both our hearts and our minds. Do you tend to lean in one direction, valuing the heart more than the mind or vice versa?

Parting Prayer

Lord, thank you for giving us such easy access to the Bible. Make us like the noble Bereans of Acts 17, receiving the word with all eagerness and examining the Scriptures daily. As we do this, please fill us with the knowledge of your will in all spiritual wisdom and understanding, so as to walk in a manner worthy of you and for your glory.

Honor *My* Parents?

———————— ·⫸||⫷· ————————

Honor your father and your mother, as the Lord your God commanded you, so that your days may be long and that it may go well with you in the land that the Lord your God is giving you.

—DEUT. 5:16

When we previously reflected on Exodus 20:12, some readers undoubtedly thought: "You expect me to honor *my* parents?" The unfortunate reality in this sin-filled world is that many of us have parents who are not worthy of honor by conventional standards. Myriad reasons could leave us feeling resentful or bitter toward one or both of our parents and make the command to "honor your mother and father" difficult to accept. Yet, there it is. So, what do we do?

First, we must recognize that all people are worthy of honor simply because they carry in themselves the image of God (Gen. 1:28). James alludes to this reality when he warns us about the dangers of the tongue: "With it we bless our Lord and Father, and with it we curse those who are made in the likeness of God . . . this ought not to be so" (James 3:9–10). In the same way, dishonoring our parents, who are made in the likeness of God, ought not to be so.

Second, we are called to honor those who are in authority over us. Paul tells us that those in authority are ultimately placed there by God (Rom. 13:1). Peter goes beyond the simple recognition of God-instituted authority and tells us to *"honor the emperor"* (1 Pet. 2:17). Difficult as this may be for some, consider David's disposition toward Saul as an example for us. Although Saul continually sought to kill him, David treated Saul with honor simply because he was anointed by God (1 Sam. 24:6–7). Just as Peter didn't choose the emperor and David didn't choose Saul, so we, who did not choose our parents, are expected to show them honor.

Last, Peter makes a blanket statement concerning the servants of God: We are called to honor *everyone* (1 Pet. 2:16–17). Jesus similarly said we shouldn't just love those who love us; instead, we should also love and pray for those who make our lives difficult (Matt. 5:43–48). So, how to apply this? As shown in the entry on Exodus 20:12, honoring and showing love to a parent who makes us feel resentful doesn't mean showering them with false praise. Instead, we begin by recognizing that they are made in God's image and that God ordained them to be our parents. Next, we heed Paul's advice in Philippians 4:8 by thinking about what is true, honorable, and lovely in our parents. We can then verbalize these things to them.

Parting Reflection

Different people feel honored differently. Some appreciate expressions of gratefulness for what they see as their due recognition. Others feel respected simply when we ask for their advice or opinion on pressing matters. What makes your mother, father, or other parental figures feel valued? Take a few minutes to think about it, write your thoughts down, and apply what you discover.

Parting Prayer

Lord, we recognize that it's not always easy to show honor to those whom we deem unworthy of it. We confess that too often we fail in this regard. Yet, we fall on your mercy and ask that you help us to honor your name by showing honor to others.

Disciplining without Degrading

———————— ·⫶⫶⫶· ————————

Forty lashes may be given but not more; if more lashes than these are given, your neighbor will be degraded in your sight.

—DEUT. 25:3

According to modern ideals, a law *should* equally apply to everyone regardless of their social status. For many in the ancient world, equality under the law was not even considered an ideal to imagine. Various ancient law codes explicitly dictated consequences for offenses based on social rank. Penalties were assessed based on the status of the offender and the offended. This isn't describing the unjust application of the law; instead, the law itself encoded social standards of honor and shame. By design, laws stipulated that someone of higher social rank could receive a lighter punishment than a lower-status person despite committing the same offense. Compared to citizens, law-breaking foreigners were often subject to the momentary whims of a local official.

By contrast, the law of Moses establishes legal equality for all, *even* foreigners. This is the revolutionary intent of the principle *lex talionis* ("eye for an eye, tooth for a tooth," Deut. 19:18–21). It treats the lowly with honor; it expresses mercy. When outsiders and low-status people do wrong, they ought not to suffer the shame of unjust punishments that the social elites avoid. Various passages such as Leviticus 24:17–22, clarify God's heart: "You shall have the same rule for the sojourner and for the native, for I am the Lord your God" (Lev. 24:22 ESV).

From this discussion, two observations jump out. First, although many theologians emphasize legal metaphors, these are not inherently sacred; the law is just one metaphor among others. Laws can be just or unjust, and they encode social ideas about honor and shame. Second, the Mosaic Law upheld and defended the honor of God's image-bearers. Even in its prescribed punishments, it protected people from excessive shaming. By ancient standards,

Deuteronomy 25:3 (quoted above) was intended to guard the offender's dignity. The goals of such actions were correction and, ultimately, restoration. The law did not use shame primarily as a weapon to degrade people.

Scripture challenges us to consider afresh the rules we make for our homes and organizations. Popular ideas about justice are often linked more to punishment and shame than restoration and honor. Consequently, we may be prone to overlook the intent of the Mosaic Law and the opportunity we have to bless others in our own families, organizations, and societies.

Parting Reflection

How might laws and policies show partiality based on social status? Where do such rules foster either honor or shame? Also, how do we enact discipline or correction without degrading others?

Parting Prayer

Thank you, Lord, for your kindness, as shown in the law of Moses. We agree with the psalmist, who prays, "O that my ways may be steadfast in keeping your statutes! Then I shall not be put to shame, having my eyes fixed on all your commandments" (Ps. 119:5–6).

Giving God Glory?

———————— ᚗᚗᚗ ————————

*Then Joshua said to Achan, "My son, give glory to the Lord God of
Israel and make confession to him. Tell me now what you have done;
do not hide it from me."*

—JOSH. 7:19

Isn't God inherently glorious and worthy of honor? This question often comes
from people worried about any language suggesting we can give God "face"
or that he might "lose face." To this, we answer with another question: What
does it mean to "give God glory"? After all, the Bible frequently beckons
people to give glory to the Lord (1 Sam. 6:5; Jer. 13:16; Rev. 14:7).

God's glory is undoubtedly infinite and unchanging, yet we don't always
recognize it. In "giving" glory to God, people do not bestow something on
God that he lacks. Instead, they profess his unique worth. Notice the words
of Isaiah 42:12, "Let them *give glory* to the Lord, and *declare his praise* in the
coastlands" (emphasis added). When we give God "face," we publicly honor
him as God (Rom. 1:19–21). One simply acknowledges what is already true.

While we might first think of singing hymns or worship songs, there are
countless ways to give God glory, honor, or face. In Joshua 7, Achan directly
disobeys the Lord by stealing things meant to be devoted to God. Therefore,
Joshua invites him to glorify God by confessing his sin (Josh. 7:19). We see
a similar connection in Revelation 16:9, concerning those who experienced
God's wrath: "They cursed the name of God, who had authority over these
plagues, and they did not repent and give him glory." A reluctance to repent
correlates to an unwillingness to give God glory.

Even Christians can misunderstand what it means to give God glory.
Many parents, pastors, and other leaders may be reluctant to admit their
sin, faults, or perhaps even their struggles. They identify their status with
God's and suppose they are protecting his reputation when, in fact, they are
simply trying to save face themselves. One pastor in China told me, "How

can I admit I don't know something [in the Bible]? It would take away my church's confidence in God."

Christ's followers are prone to forget that we often must "lose face" to give him face. We need to confess our sin, weakness, and need for him; otherwise, we profess our self-sufficiency. We essentially proclaim to the world that we do not need God. We do not give God glory by honoring ourselves. It's only in giving God glory that we gain true honor, which he bestows on us through Christ.

Parting Reflection

How might you confuse God's honor and protecting your reputation? How should this insight change your life when you understand the relationship between confession and glorifying the Lord?

Parting Prayer

"Not to us, O Lord, not to us, but to your name give glory" (Ps. 115:1). Father, we admit our tendency to think more about our reputation than yours. Spirit, open our eyes and change our hearts to give you glory by confessing our failures and needs.

Whom Will They Remember?

⎯⎯⎯⎯⎯⎯⎯⎯ ⑈⑈⑈ ⎯⎯⎯⎯⎯⎯⎯⎯

He [Gideon] responded [to the Lord], "But sir, how can I deliver Israel?
My clan is the weakest in Manasseh, and I am the least in my family."

—JUDG. 6:15

Gideon's service as a judge of Israel mirrors the path of many today who seek to do the Lord's ministry. Both triumph and tragedy mark his career. Judges 6–8 tells not only of the rise and fall of a nation's fortunes but also of reputations.

Gideon's status raises when he boldly destroys the altar of Baal. But his work is not primarily about himself. Instead, it is for God's renown. When confronted, his father Joash says, "If he [Baal] is a god, let him contend for himself, because his altar has been pulled down" (Judg. 6:31). The Lord then uses a meager force of just 300 men to rescue Israel from the Midianites. But why does God want Gideon to use so few men? Well, the Lord says, "The troops with you are too many for me to give the Midianites into their hand. Israel would only take the credit away from me, saying, 'My own hand has delivered me'" (Judg. 7:2). Put simply, the Lord wants the glory when he achieves great things through Gideon's ministry.

Gideon says all the right things, as when he tells the Israelites, "I will not rule over you, and my son will not rule over you; the Lord will rule over you" (Judg. 8:23). However, what Gideon does matters more than what he says. He immediately makes a gold ephod, which culturally is seen as another path to God, separate from the tabernacle. Resting in Gideon's house, this ephod fosters an alternative "spirituality" that ensnares the people by minimizing the Lord's way. The people try using Gideon to access the Lord's blessings without seeking the Lord himself.

Gideon unwisely serves in a way that seems right to him but ultimately leads to shame. When he dies, "the Israelites relapsed and prostituted themselves with the Baals, making Baal-Berith their god. The Israelites did not remember the Lord their God . . . and they did not exhibit loyalty to [Gideon]" (Judg. 8:33–35).

In doing great things for God, we must seek to work with him, in his way, and in his timing. Gideon confuses the people's loyalty to him with their having faith in the Lord. We want people to remember Christ. Yet, when we conflate our gain with God's glory, our actions dishonor the Lord, and we entice people away from him.

Parting Reflection

How do you measure success as a follower of Christ? In what ways might you mistake the attention of others with their giving honor to God?

Parting Prayer

Lord, we who serve you are tempted to undermine our words with our actions. We often mistakenly think a good reputation means that we are getting kingdom results. Make us who you call us to be, doing what you call us to do, in your ways, and in your timing.

The Reputation of Ruth

—|||||—

[Ruth] said to him, "Why have I found favor in your eyes, that you should take notice of me, since I am a foreigner?" But Boaz answered her, "All that you have done for your mother-in-law since the death of your husband has been fully told to me, and how you left your father and mother and your native land and came to a people that you did not know before."

—RUTH 2:10–11 ESV

Upon returning to Israel, Ruth and Naomi have little going for them. Besides suffering from famine and tragedies, these women likely endure the contempt of their neighbors. Naomi calls herself "Mara" (meaning "bitter") and claims, "the Lord has testified against me and the Almighty has brought calamity upon me" (Ruth 1:21 ESV). Ruth is a Moabite foreigner, whom Israel disdains and excludes (Deut. 23:3–6). Nevertheless, Ruth dares to seek help by gleaning and gathering the sheaves after the reapers in Boaz's field. While the Lord allows for this in Leviticus 23:22, that provision does not alleviate the long-held prejudices by Israelites against Moabites (e.g., Num. 22–24). Who is this woman to think that she should benefit alongside native Israelites?

What distinguishes Ruth in the eyes of Boaz? Her reputation. She forsakes an easier path in life to show loyalty to Naomi and entrust herself to the Lord (Ruth 1:11–16; 2:12). In traditional, honor-shame-oriented cultures, perhaps nothing is more honorable than demonstrating loyalty to one's family. Boaz shares this value, as will become explicit in Ruth 3–4. Ruth 2 suggests that Boaz is aware that Ruth is family since she is related to Naomi (Ruth 2:1, 3, 6).

So, what does Boaz do? Because Ruth proves herself to be an honorable woman, he makes sure that his workers treat her accordingly. Boaz orders his men not to harass her or humiliate her (Ruth 2:9, 15). Furthermore, he goes well beyond polite niceties by providing for her in abundance. He even commands the young men, "You must also pull out some handfuls for her from the bundles, and leave them for her to glean, and do not rebuke her" (Ruth 2:16).

Knowing the importance of her reputation, Ruth risks it for the sake of loving Naomi (Ruth 3). Following Naomi's instructions, Ruth makes a respectful, indirect appeal for Boaz to marry her. However, Ruth's approach could easily be misunderstood as a scandalous attempt to seduce him. She makes herself vulnerable to rejection and gossip, yet Boaz once again recognizes her exceedingly honorable act of loyalty (Ruth 3:10). Therefore, he commits to redeeming Ruth and Naomi and their family name. As a result, "The women said to Naomi, 'Blessed be the Lord, who has not left you this day without next-of-kin; and may his name be renowned in Israel!'" (Ruth 4:14). After returning to Israel in disgrace, the community now esteems Naomi because of the honorable and faith-filled actions that gave Ruth a reputation worth noticing.

Parting Reflection

In our age, people often see relationships as merely transactional. Loyalty becomes too inconvenient when times get tough. In your relationships, how might you demonstrate true honor, as Ruth showed toward Naomi?

Parting Prayer

Besides you, Father, no one has shown greater steadfast love and kindness. You invite us to take refuge under your wings (Ruth 2:12). Spirit, embolden us to remain faithful even when we face hardship and others reject us.

Dealing with Shame

──────── ⫸ ────────

Her rival used to provoke her severely, to irritate her, because the Lord
had closed her womb . . . Therefore Hannah wept and would not eat.

—1 SAM. 1:6–7

In biblical times, a woman's ability to bear children was highly valued. As a result, barrenness carried with it a deep sense of shame. Throughout Scripture, barren women react to this stigma. Sarah says of Hagar, "When she saw that she had conceived, she looked on me with contempt" (Gen. 16:5). Rachel's barrenness causes her to envy her sister, exclaiming to Jacob, "Give me children, or I shall die" (Gen. 30:1)! When God then opens her womb and she bears Joseph, Rachel says, "God has taken away my reproach" (Gen. 30:23).

Hannah's story also displays the shame of barrenness, along with an admirable response to it. Elkanah has two wives. The first, Hannah, is barren and has no children. The second, Peninnah, has children. Peninnah regularly ridicules Hannah because of her barrenness. "So it went on year by year; as often as she went up to the house of the Lord, she [Peninnah] used to provoke her. Therefore Hannah wept and would not eat" (1 Sam. 1:7). The scorn that Hannah feels leaves her in despair, yet she doesn't dwell in it. The following verses show her response.

While Hannah is in prayer, the high priest, Eli, mistakes her for a drunken woman and rebukes her. Hannah responds, showing how she deals with her felt shame, "I have been pouring out my soul before the Lord. Do not regard your servant as a worthless woman, for I have been speaking out of my great anxiety and vexation all this time" (1 Sam. 1:15–16). She doesn't ignore her feelings, nor does she put up a façade. Instead, she entrusts herself to the Lord in prayer, believing that he can reverse her shame. When Samuel is born, Hannah responds with worshipful prayer. She begins and ends her song with the recognition that the Lord alone exalts and gives honor (1 Sam. 2:1, 10). Throughout, she rejoices in God's salvation and his authority over all things.

Like Hannah, we should take our feelings of shame and reproach to the Lord in prayer. While we may not see a miracle in this life as she did, we know that many years later, another woman who conceived a child in an even more unlikely manner sang a song bearing a striking resemblance to Hannah's song (Luke 1:46–55). This son, Jesus Christ, would remove shame and provide honor for eternity to those who trust in him.

Parting Reflection

Is there anything in your life that leaves you feeling like you're in a perpetual state of shame? Perhaps a disability, limitation, or some other physical characteristic that you wish you could change. What would it look like to entrust yourself to the Lord in prayer as Hannah did?

Parting Prayer

God, we praise you for being the only one who can overcome our shame. Jesus, thank you for securing for us an eternity with you in your glory. Like Hannah, help our hearts to exult in you and to rejoice in your salvation.

Basking in the Glory of the Lord

---- ⑈ ----

> *But Michal the daughter of Saul came out to meet David, and said,*
> *"How the king of Israel honored himself today, uncovering himself*
> *today before the eyes of his servants' maids, as any vulgar fellow might*
> *shamelessly uncover himself!" David said to Michal, . . . "I have danced*
> *before the Lord. I will make myself yet more contemptible than this,*
> *and I will be abased in my own eyes; but by the maids of whom you*
> *have spoken, by them I shall be held in honor."*
>
> —2 SAM. 6:20–23

The dramatic events of 2 Samuel 6 interweave a concern for holiness and honor. After Uzzah is struck down for his irreverent handling of the ark of God,[22] David returns to bring the ark to Jerusalem. This time, they are careful to properly honor the ark as they transport it (6:13–15). They shout for joy on their journey, understanding that the ark signifies God's presence in David's kingdom. The king dances with all his might, jubilantly worshiping God as he whirls around in his linen ephod. Undoubtedly, this was a moment of pure elation.

Enter Michal. Interestingly, the author identifies her as "the daughter of Saul" instead of as David's wife. This is deliberate and suggests that, like her father, she too lacks spiritual discernment. We learn that Michal "despised [David] in her heart" (6:16). So, when David comes to bless his household, Michal sarcastically remarks, "How the king of Israel has honored himself today" (6:20). While no root is pinpointed, she is seeping with bitterness toward David. This blinds her to the honor and joy that should have been hers as a member of God's community on this blessed day.

---

22. See the entry for 1 Chronicles 13:9–10 for a fuller explanation of this event.

Instead, she accuses the king of Israel of dancing shamefully and dishonoring his role by not wearing his royal robes as she supposed he should. David refuses to let her words ruin the moment, insisting that his primary concern is how the Lord views him. If celebrating God's blessing brings disgrace, he is willing to make himself *"more contemptible than this"* (6:22). David and the people of God revel in the glory of the Lord, honoring him with all of their hearts, minds, and bodies. In contrast, Michal sulks alone and allows the bitterness to fester. She refuses to enjoy God's glory and receive the honor signified by the ark's arrival in Jerusalem.

Joy in the Lord is not rooted in our outward circumstances, but in recognizing the honor that God bestows on us. In his great mercy, Jesus reconciles us to God and gives us a glorious inheritance that is *"imperishable, undefiled, and unfading"* (1 Pet. 1:4). What honor he gives to us! So, as we look to the cross, let us bask in the glory of Christ and all that belonging to him means for us.

Parting Reflection

Meditating about what God has accomplished on our behalf is one way to recognize the honor that God bestows on us. Peter says the inheritance that Christ has for us is "imperishable, undefiled, and unfading." Take a few moments and meditate on each of those terms. What does each mean? And as you reflect, be sure to bask in the glory of the Lord.

Parting Prayer

Lord, you alone are holy. Help us to revere you as we should. As we seek your face, help us to sever all roots of bitterness that choke out our joy in you.

David and Uriah

──────────── ·◁▷· ────────────

It happened, late one afternoon.

—2 SAM. 11:2

Second Samuel 11 is one of the most shocking chapters in the entire Bible. It begins with David's dereliction of his duty as king to go out to war with the rest of his army. Then comes a tragic series of events that results in David's illicit interaction with Bathsheba, perhaps bribing Uriah to know his wife, and when he doesn't do so, having Uriah killed in battle. Outrageous! How could David be so callous? To better understand this story, let's acknowledge a few points that Westerners typically miss.

First, David's sexual sin is not a private matter; it is public. Notice that David sends several messengers to bring Bathsheba to the palace. Also, when Bathsheba discovers that she's pregnant, she likewise sends messengers to inform David. Undoubtedly, the news about their encounter and resulting pregnancy spread quickly throughout the palace. Additionally, when David summons Uriah, it may seem like only David and Bathsheba know about the pregnancy and that David tries to dupe an unwitting Uriah in order to make everyone else think the baby was conceived in wedlock. However, this is very unlikely—everyone would have known that David was responsible for the pregnancy, most likely including Uriah by the time he arrived home.

So, what's David's angle here? In short, David tries to save face and preserve his honor by making it appear that Uriah is the baby's father. Richards and O'Brien explain, "David is asking Uriah to let him off the hook. If Uriah comes home and spends one night with his wife, then the baby is 'technically' Uriah's, even though everyone knows otherwise. Honor would be restored."[23]

───────────────

23. E. Randolph Richards and Brandon J. O'Brien, *Misreading Scripture with Western Eyes: Removing Our Cultural Blinders to Better Understand the Bible* (Downers Grove, IL: IVP Academic, 2013), 123.

In fact, David even juices his request by sending Uriah a gift (2 Sam. 11:8). Yet, Uriah won't play along and effectively shames David by not going to his home despite David's repeated requests. Furthermore, he doesn't keep his refusal private but makes it public by sleeping at the door of the king's house (2 Sam. 11:9). To preserve his honor, David retaliates by having Uriah killed. As much as it may upset Western sensibilities, everything David does here is "typical for a Mediterranean king at the time in a situation like this. And according to the honor and shame system of David's day, the matter was resolved."[24]

None of this excuses David's behavior. Scripture is clear that God was not pleased with David (2 Sam. 11:27). However, this does help to better understand the role that honor and shame play both in 2 Samuel 11 and in many cultural contexts today.

Parting Reflection

Have you previously considered how honor and shame shape 2 Samuel 11? Spend a few minutes thinking about the implications of this interpretation. Whereas David's behavior displeased God, how did the one true king, Jesus, use his power?

Parting Prayer

Have mercy on us, sinners, for we all are prone to behave in contradictory ways. On the one hand, we work to build and protect our status. On the other, we live as though the values we espouse in public matter little to us. We are ashamed and confess the truth to you. Spirit, grant us humility and resilience to pursue genuine godliness.

---

24. Richards and O'Brien, 125.

David and Nathan

———————— ⑾⑾⑾ ————————

Nathan said to David, "You are the man!"

—2 SAM. 12:7

King David's actions in 2 Samuel 11 were not entirely unexpected given the cultural standards of the time. David most likely thought that the matter was resolved when he had Uriah killed. But was it?

Even though David felt that the matter was resolved, "The thing that David had done displeased the Lord" (2 Sam. 11:27). We may wonder why David felt no remorse about what he did. His conscience almost certainly was not driven by the inner turmoil that comes with feeling guilty. More likely, he was driven by a more external mode of conviction brought about by shame. Richards and O'Brien are helpful:

> David doesn't appear to be experiencing any inner pressure. No matter. God is not stymied by culture. God had introduced another element into ancient Near Eastern culture: a prophet. Instead of a voice whispering into his heart, a prophet shouted at his face. Either way, God speaks. Since David's culture used shame to bring about conformity, God used shame to bring David to repentance.[25]

And so, God sends the prophet Nathan to confront the king. He shows David that he is not merely accountable to the cultural standards of his day, but more importantly to God's universal standards for righteousness. First, David's sexual offense was a clear violation of God's law. Second, David's abuse of power as king would not be given a pass. So, what does God, using the prophet Nathan to convict David, teach us? For one and as noted above,

_____

25. Richards and O'Brien, 126.

culture will never be an excuse to avoid repentance. God transcends culture. His authority is universal, and his ability to reconcile people to himself cannot be thwarted by any culture.

Finally, God pronounces judgment on David because of his transgressions, yet comforts him by saying through Nathan, "The Lord has also put away your sin" (2 Sam. 12:13). But how? Whereas David abused his power, Jesus gives a clear picture of how a true king should act in Mark 10:42–45:

> *You know that among the Gentiles those whom they recognize as their rulers lord it over them, and their great ones are tyrants over them. But it is not so among you; but whoever wishes to become great among you must be your servant, . . . For even the Son of Man came not to be served but to serve, and to give his life a ransom for many.*

Parting Reflection

Many ancient people expected kings to have their way, even if immoral, so long as they hid their behavior and protected their honor. Take a few minutes to think about how different cultures may feel convicted of wrongdoing. Think first within your own culture or generation, perhaps Generation Z compared to Baby Boomers. Next, think more broadly, comparing two countries with vastly different cultures. How do these standards of honor differ from the Lord's?

Parting Prayer

Spirit, you convict us of wrongdoing, but we confess that our hearts can be insensitive to your prodding. When we turn away, send people like Nathan into our lives. Soften our hearts so that we would not be shameless and help us to honor you and those around us.

Dedicating the Temple

———————— ⑈ ————————

Hear in heaven your dwelling place, and do according to all that the foreigner calls to you, so that all the peoples of the earth may know your name and fear you, as do your people Israel.

—1 KINGS 8:43

Why does God rescue Israel from Egypt? It concerns more than just their political freedom. Arriving in the promised land of Canaan also is not the climax of God's plan in the Old Testament. Instead, it's the building of the Temple, where God's glorious presence would reside among his people. This is the place in which the Lord says, "My name shall be there" (1 Kings 8:29).

After many years of preparation, Solomon dedicates the Temple to the Lord with extended prayer (1 Kings 8; 2 Chron. 6). Through it, we learn more about God's mission and that of his people in the world. In this prayer, we see how the Lord intends to bring honor to himself. First, he is a promise keeper who ensures that his word is fulfilled, even if it takes generations (1 Kings 8:23–26). Second, the Lord is unlike other ancient gods, who remain distant, unconcerned, and sometimes temperamental. The Creator God graciously draws near to his people (1 Kings 8:27–30). Third, he delights in showing mercy. God is not surprised by our flaws and failings, but compassionately forgives sin (1 Kings 8:31–34, 46–52). Fourth, he sovereignly answers prayers when people seek deliverance from affliction (1 Kings 8:35–40, 44–45).

Finally, the Lord distinguishes himself as the one true God of all nations (1 Kings 8:41–43). He is not a provincial deity, limited in concern or the scope of his domain. It is here that we discern why God reveals himself in these ways. Solomon reinforces God's ultimate reason for the Temple: "so that all the peoples of the earth may know the Lord is God and there is no other" (1 Kings 8:60).

In all this, we catch a glimpse of the church's mission, especially what it means for Christ's people to be called God's temple (1 Cor. 3:16–17). We are called to bring honor to him in all the world, drawing near to outsiders, extending forgiveness, and working to provide for those who are suffering. Christ's followers bring him glory by remaining faithful. Even in weakness, we can seek to know Christ and make his name known.

Parting Reflection

Even if you feel as though you have low status or that your failings disqualify you from approaching God, he is honored in ways that are both countercultural and counterintuitive. What are some ways that you can glorify God from a position of weakness?

Parting Prayer

With Solomon, we pray:

> *The Lord our God be with us, as he was with our ancestors; may he not leave us or abandon us, but incline our hearts to him, to walk in all his ways, and to keep his commandments, his statutes, and his ordinances, which he commanded our ancestors.*
> —1 Kings 8:57–58

Touching the Ark of God

———————— ⦙⦙⦙ ————————

*Uzzah put out his hand to hold the ark, for the oxen shook it. The anger
of the Lord was kindled against Uzzah; he struck him down because
he put out his hand to the ark; and he died there before God.*

—1 CHRON. 13:9–10

At the height of the American Civil War, Confederate William Mumford
tore down the American flag and dragged it through the streets in protest.
Shortly after, Mumford was executed for desecrating the nation's flag. Why
such a severe punishment? Notice how a Union general denounced the confederate mob:

> They have *insulted* our flag—torn it down with *indignity*. This outrage will
> be punished in such a manner as in my judgment will caution both the per-
> petrators and abettors of the act, so that they will fear the stripes, *if they do
> not reverence the stars of our banner.*[26]

People intuitively grasp what it means to treat something as sacred, worthy
of unique honor. Still, readers are often perplexed by God striking down Uzzah
when he touches the ark. "Isn't God a bit uptight?" some ask. Unlike national
flags, which are owned and flown by people throughout the world, the ark
uniquely serves as the symbolic *throne for God.*[27] No wonder the Lord gave
such specific instructions about how to carry it (Exod. 25:12–14).

Yet, David's men transport the ark by cart, just as they would anything
else. They intend to honor God and bring him worship. Instead, they treat

---

26. "862: William B. Mumford, flag desecrator." 7 July 2009. Online: https://www.executed
today.com/2009/06/07/1862-william-b-mumford-flag-desecrator/
27. Cf. Scripture passages such as 1 Chronicles 13:6, 1 Samuel 4:4, and 2 Kings 19:15.

his throne with casual neglect. When Uzzah sees the oxen stumble, horror no doubt courses through his body as he anticipates the ark being defiled by mud. How shameful to let God's throne descend to the earthen filth below!

Uzzah, however, has a fundamental misunderstanding about how to honor God. He assumes that the ground below is dirtier than his own hand. Uzzah forgets that he is a broken sinner, tainted by sin save for the mercy of God. He mistakes the call of God, who does not delight in mere ritual but reverence. The various sacrifices and rituals of worship are simply expressions of godly devotion. In reality, Uzzah's blood stains the hands of David and the assembly. Uzzah's error is rooted in an increasingly casual attitude toward God that pre-dated the day of his death. He belonged to a community that treated what is holy as though it were common. In profaning God in this way, they provoke the Lord and disgrace themselves. Uzzah's death befits a cavalier attitude toward God's holiness. Let us not be so casual in our service to God.

Parting Reflection

How might you be too casual in how you worship God and follow Christ? What is the relationship between ritual and reverence?

Parting Prayer

Lord, thank you for the sobering story of 1 Chronicles 13–15. We long for more than casual religion. You desire that our hearts would worship, like David, with great dancing and celebration. Teach us to honor you with all our minds, hearts, and bodies.

Should We Care About Reputation?

─────────── ⑂ ───────────

Then I perceived and saw that God had not sent him at all, but he had pronounced the prophecy against me because Tobiah and Sanballat had hired him. He was hired for this purpose, to intimidate me and make me sin by acting in this way, and so they could give me a bad name, in order to taunt me.

—NEH. 6:12–13

God called Nehemiah and the returned exiles to a special task. Many years after Jerusalem's destruction, rebuilding the wall around that city would be a supernatural work. They could expect opposition from God's enemies. These enemies used a sinister tactic—attacking Nehemiah's reputation. First, Sanballat accuses Nehemiah of rebelling against King Artaxerxes. When that plan fails, the enemies of God attempt to make Nehemiah run away and so ruin his own name (Neh. 6:11). Therefore, they hire a false prophet to spread lies, saying people seek to kill Nehemiah. Tobiah and Sanballat want Nehemiah to be so afraid that he disobeys God's calling.

When we are following God's call, people may attack us, trying to disparage our good name. They will use our natural desire for a good reputation as a weapon against us. That does not mean, however, that we should ignore or be indifferent to reputation. Consider when Nehemiah's enemies heard that the people finished the wall. "All the nations around us were afraid and fell greatly in their own esteem; for they perceived that this work had been accomplished with the help of our God" (Neh. 6:16).

Nehemiah persevered in his calling and finished rebuilding the wall because he didn't play the same status games that his enemies played. Rather, Nehemiah understood that God's renown is of utmost importance, not his own reputation. Nehemiah cares about his own name only inasmuch as it serves the purposes of God. So, how do we have the resilience needed to see God do extraordinary things in our lives? In part, we refuse to compete and compare ourselves based on the approval of social influencers; instead, we seek only to accomplish what brings glory to God.

By contrast, what happens when the fear of losing face or status begins to consume us? We take shortcuts or compromise in following God's call. We set up walls in an attempt to hide our secrets. By doing this, we slowly build a bad reputation that is difficult to tear down. Instead, let us be like Nehemiah, who is not worried about the lies and insults heaped on him by others. His integrity will vindicate him. Nehemiah's sense of responsibility before God is greater than his regard for the opinion of the crowd.

Parting Reflection

Our reputations can be ruined when people accuse us of wrongdoing or misunderstand our motives. We sometimes face that threat when trying to do the right thing. When have you been scared to do what is right because of what others might think of you? On the other hand, do we give people legitimate reasons to discredit us?

Parting Prayer

God, you are the giver of all wisdom. We plead for discernment to perceive the motives of our hearts. We ask for resilience to persevere when our reputations are unjustly threatened. You are worthy of all praise, for you know the truth and will reveal what is in the human heart.

Who Cares If I'm Innocent?

———————— ·⫴⫴⫴· ————————

If I am guilty, woe to me! If I am in the right, I cannot lift up my head,
for I am filled with disgrace and look on my affliction.

—JOB 10:15 ESV

Mike had long dreamed of a career in counseling, desiring to help people in the church who were overlooked, especially those who came from challenging childhoods. One day, his girlfriend reported to their university that he had assaulted her. School officials promptly put him on probation, and his network of friends dissipated very quickly. However, within a few weeks, Mike's then-former girlfriend publicly admitted that she had made it all up. She had been angry, but her accusation had exacted lasting damage. Feeling isolated, Mike languished in depression, eventually dropped out of college, and gave up on his long-desired career goals. For Mike, it didn't matter that he was innocent. In the court of public opinion, he was guilty until proven innocent.

A comment was shared on social media. A public remark made by someone with influence. At best, such words cast a veil of doubt on a person's character and reputation. At worst, they destroy a lifetime of hard work, even one's life. In the court of public opinion, injustice can be swift and sure. These dynamics are nothing new. Job experienced a harsh and hasty judgment from his friends, compounding his already wretched condition. It did not matter that he was innocent. The relational pain was so severe that he would not be consoled even knowing he was "righteous" (Job 10:15). Why? He is saturated with shame.

For countless people, guilt and innocence are not their primary concerns. Even if they are innocent, the disgrace inflicted on them makes them despair of life. Jeremiah preferred not being born rather than continuing to endure humiliation. He asks, "Why did I come forth from the womb to see toil and sorrow, and spend my days in shame" (Jer. 20:18)?

Shame is one consequence of sin, but that shame is not always felt by the one who sins. In the case of Job, his suffering was not due to his failure (Job 1–2). Instead, it was due to Job being dishonored by his friends. It was *their* sin that caused him shame. Their insistence on proving Job guilty or wrong blinded them to the injustice they imposed on him. Sadly, they managed only to provoke Job to grow more defensive. For this, the Lord finally rebukes Job, "Will you even put me in the wrong? Will you condemn me that you may be justified?" (Job 40:8). Shame is not always the result of specific sins, but being shamed by others can lead someone to sin.

Parting Reflection

When have you felt socially shamed because people treated you as if you were "guilty until proven innocent"? How might those experiences help you adjust how you treat and speak about others?

Parting Prayer

Father, you want us to be innocent of wrongdoing, but that includes the sins of hasty speech and ill-informed accusations. Spirit, we need your help when we are slandered. Guard our hearts so that we would not be discouraged and fall into sin. Thank you, Jesus, for your example of patient endurance.

Seeking God's Face

———————— ⫻ ————————

They will receive blessing from the Lord, and vindication from the God of their salvation. Such is the company of those who seek him, who seek the face of the God of Jacob.

—PS. 24:5–6

How do we seek God's face? Is it merely a spiritual activity, or are other facets of our lives involved? Psalm 24 can help us out.

Psalm 24:3 asks two rhetorical questions, "Who shall ascend the hill of the Lord? And who shall stand in his holy place?" These questions remind us that not everyone will receive God's blessing. Ascending a hill implies struggle and difficulty. Remember Genesis 32, where Jacob only received God's blessing after he wrestled with him all night? Let's not assume that we are seeking God's face; instead, let's acknowledge our shortcomings and examine ourselves regularly. We can do so briefly by looking at the following verses, which provide answers to those rhetorical questions.

First, the one who seeks God's face has "clean hands and pure hearts" (Ps. 24:4). To have "clean hands" hints at outward and practical holiness, while "pure hearts" suggest proper motives. These two are deeply connected. As Charles Spurgeon noted, "There must be a work of grace in the core of the heart as well as in the palm of the hand, or our religion is a delusion."[28] Are you seeking God's face with both your internal thoughts and external actions?

Second, seeking God's face means to be one "who does not trust in an idol or swear by a false god" (Ps. 24:4 NIV). We must not be in love with the corruption of this world. Countless potential idols vie for our allegiance in this life, yet only God is supreme. We must seek first his kingdom. Do you

---

28. C. H. Spurgeon, *The Treasury of David,* https://archive.spurgeon.org/treasury/treasury .php.

seek God's face while being aware of potential idols in your life, continually renouncing them, and daily committing yourself to worship God alone?

Third, those who seek God's face "will receive blessing from the Lord, and vindication from the God of their salvation" (Ps. 24:5). Blessing and righteousness are not things we earn from God. Instead, true saints "do not ascend the hill of the Lord as givers but as receivers, and they do not wear their own merits, but a righteousness which they have received."[29] Are you seeking God's face while allowing him to empower and cleanse you from sin?

Ultimately, seeking God's face goes beyond waking up early in the morning to read Scripture or setting aside specific times to pray. It includes those things, but it is also a holistic striving for God that involves both our internal thoughts and external actions. To seek God's face is to make a resolute commitment to actively pursue God's honor in every facet of our lives.

Parting Reflection

If we're honest, none of us pass this examination. Each day, we fail on each point. But just as David wrote in Psalm 24:7–10, let's lift up our heads to see this King of glory to whom the ancient doors open up— Jesus Christ.

Parting Prayer

Lord, we know that you are infinitely glorious and worthy of everything that we have. We confess that we do not always seek your face as we should. Empower us to seek your face by walking in a manner worthy of and fully pleasing to you.

---

29. Spurgeon, *Treasury of David.*

Glorifying God by Giving Thanks

————— ⑃ —————

Those who bring thanksgiving as their sacrifice honor me.

—PS. 50:23

When we think of how to glorify God, our first thoughts may be about doing certain actions, singing worship songs, or just having a strong faith. Perhaps we respond with a catch-all phrase, saying we seek to honor God in all that we do. Those are certainly good answers and worthy of meditation. Beyond those, however, Psalm 50:23 offers another way that we can honor God— by giving thanks.

How does showing gratitude glorify God? Well, gratefulness is the proper response to God's work in our lives and points others to him. Charles Spurgeon vibrantly elaborates:

> Though nothing can add the least cubit to God's essential glory, yet praise exalts him in the eyes of others. Praise is a setting forth of God's honor, a lifting up of his name, a displaying the trophy of his goodness, a proclaiming his excellency, a spreading his renown, a breaking open the box of ointment, whereby the sweet savor and perfume of God's name is sent abroad into the world.[30]

Giving thanks to God is not simply a private matter. It also has a public dimension and should be noticed by those we regularly interact with.

Paul makes a similar connection in 2 Corinthians 4:13, saying that his knowledge of God brings about his belief, which is then expressed in his speaking: "I believed and so I spoke." Paul's faith in Christ compels him to proclaim the resurrected Jesus who is reconciling the world to himself for the

---

30. Spurgeon, *The Treasury of David,* https://archive.spurgeon.org/treasury/treasury.php.

sake of the Corinthians "so that grace, as it extends to more and more people, may increase thanksgiving, to the glory of God" (2 Cor. 4:15).

Public thanksgiving can be a form of evangelism. Our knowledge of God and what he does for us brings about a sense of gratitude that is then expressed by offering thanksgiving. Publicly, this could include a prayer with friends before a meal or praising God for something in front of coworkers. Just as Paul said, "I believed and so I spoke," we can say, "I was grateful and so I gave thanks." And as we publicly give thanks, we send abroad into the world the perfume of God's name and we do so in the hopes that it would increase thanksgiving to the glory of God.

Parting Reflection

Do you have a habit of giving thanks to God in front of family members, friends, or colleagues? How might doing so provide opportunities to bring honor to God's name?

Parting Prayer

Father, we praise you for who you are and all that you have accomplished for us. Give us a spirit of gratefulness and the boldness to be publicly grateful to you in front of those within our sphere of influence and for your glory.

God's Face for Us

---- ⑈ ----

Do not hide your face from your servant, for I am in distress—make haste to answer me. Draw near to me, redeem me, set me free because of my enemies. You know the insults I receive, and my shame and dishonor; my foes are all known to you.

—PS. 69:17–19

In Psalm 69, David cries out for God to save him from his enemies who attack him on several fronts. He makes his plea using various images, among them the concept of "face." David asks God to not hide his face from him. The mention of "face" certainly refers to God's presence, but David seems to have more in mind with this request. For David, God not hiding his face means that he would save his people, which entails God being actively for them. Hence, at the end of this psalm, David confidently asserts that God will rebuild Judah's cities and that the people will dwell there safely.

David's request is based on two realities. First, David has indeed fulfilled his societal responsibilities to the community (69:7–9). He has attempted to do his part in keeping the covenant through prayer and worship (69:10–13, 30–33). Let's make no mistake, David is under no illusions that he is sinless (69:5). Yet, he still holds out hope that God will not hide his face but instead will turn toward him, saving him and the people. The significance of God's face being toward or for someone goes beyond having his spiritual presence; it includes God's active disposition to work for their good. What honor!

God's character is the second and primary basis of David's request. He rests in God's faithfulness, steadfast love, and abundant mercy (69:13, 16). Otherwise, David knows that he is doomed.

And such is also the case for us. The apostle Paul knew this in his bones. In Romans 8:28, he wrote of his confidence that God works all things together for the good of those that are in Christ. In other words, God's face invariably shines on those who trust in Christ. But how can this be? It is because Christ

endured the taunts of the authorities and the faithlessness of his friends
(69:8–9, 19–20). He embraced the shame of the cross, a judgment deserved
by sinners. Yet, he knew the Father would not ultimately turn his face away
from him. He would vindicate his Son by raising him from the dead. In
Romans 15:3, Paul applies to Christ the words of Psalm 69:7, which says, "It
is for your sake that I have borne reproach, that shame has covered my face."

Parting Reflection

How might you communicate the gospel in light of Christ's bearing our
shame so that the oppressed may be glad and our hearts revived (Ps. 69:32)?

Parting Prayer

One element of prayer is worship. Read the words of this well-known hymn
and turn them into prayer:

> How deep the Father's love for us,
> How vast beyond all measure,
> That he should give his only Son
> To make a wretch his treasure.
> How great the pain of searing loss—
> The Father turns his face away,
> As wounds which mar the Chosen One
> Bring many sons to glory.[31]

---

31. Stuart Townsend, "How Deep the Father's Love for Us." Stuart Townend Copyright © 1995
Thankyou Music.

Making Sense of Difficult Psalms

———————— ⑃ ————————

How long, O Lord? Will you be angry forever? Will your jealous wrath burn like fire? Pour out your anger on the nations that do not know you, and on the kingdoms that do not call on your name. For they have devoured Jacob and laid waste his habitation.

—PS. 79:5–7

If you've read through the psalms, you've undoubtedly come across several that leave you scratching your head, wondering how possibly to interpret or apply them.[32] In these difficult psalms, authors typically invoke a curse or condemnation against someone. This side of Christ, these jarring calls for vengeance appear to be the opposite of turning the other cheek or praying for one's enemies. Yet here they are, and we can't ignore them. Two points are instructive for us.

First, we must remember the oppressive environment in which the Israelites lived. We'll assume that, like us, most of our readers live what historically could be considered "safe" lives. We don't fear an invading army tearing up our community, killing many, and dragging us away to another nation in humiliation. Our modern lives of relative ease can color how we understand these psalms. But this wasn't a reality for the ancient Israelites. For many of them, oppression was not only their history in Egypt but also their present reality as exiles in Assyria and Babylon. Understandably, they longed for divine justice. Tremper Longman offers a helpful perspective for modern readers. He says, "I wonder whether our generally comfortable setting obscures our appreciation for the picture of God who comes in and 'sets things right' for

---

32. They are often called the "imprecatory psalms." Examples include Psalms 5, 10, 17, 35, 58, 59, 69, 70, 79, 83, 109, 129, 137, and 140. Compare Revelation 6:9–10.

his oppressed people — not just helping them but bringing justice on the heads of the perpetrators who have so exploited them."[33]

A second instructive point is that the vast majority of these calls for justice are made out of a concern for God's glory. Many of these invocations for judgment use the same reasoning we find in Psalm 79:7, "For they have devoured Jacob and laid waste his habitation." In essence, the psalmist calls on God to defend his name. Instead of taking matters into their own hands through physical violence, these psalms ask the Lord to execute judgment and bring Israel's enemies down to size. Honor is at stake: God's, Israel's, and their enemies'.

These two points provide a fresh lens for understanding these difficult psalms. While we may not feel comfortable praying like this, we know that at the end of the age Christ will come to "repay according to everyone's work" (Rev. 22:12). And when he does, a great status reversal will take effect for many. The oppressors will be thrown down, while the oppressed will be raised to glory in Christ.

Parting Reflection

How have you typically dealt with these difficult psalms? How do these insights help to explain some sections of Scripture that upset our modern sensibilities?

Parting Prayer

God, we know that you do not turn a blind eye to injustice. While judgment may not come as quickly as we'd like, help us to take rest knowing that you will repay all evil. Lord, we confess that we too deserve condemnation. Thank you for sending your Son, who forgives sin and reconciles us to himself and others.

---

33. Tremper Longman III, *Confronting Old Testament Controversies: Pressing Questions about Evolution, Sexuality, History, and Violence* (Grand Rapids, MI: Baker, 2019), 201.

One Purpose of Shame

———————— ⫷⫸ ————————

Fill their faces with shame . . . Let them be put to shame and dismayed forever; let them perish in disgrace.

—PS. 83:16–18

In Psalm 83, Asaph pleads with God to deliver Israel from their enemies and to bring judgment on them, part of which is to leave them in abject shame. Some of this language may be disturbing to our ears. To see more of what is going on in this passage, the shaming techniques of Chinese parents referenced in a previous entry can help us remember that one purpose of shaming in honor-shame cultures is to bring about obedience.

In quoting Psalm 83:16–18 above, portions of the text were intentionally omitted. In those sections, we see the psalmist reiterate the same purpose. He prays:

> *Fill their faces with shame,* so that they may seek your name, O Lord. *Let them be put to shame and dismayed forever; let them perish in disgrace.* Let them know that you alone, whose name is the Lord, are the Most High over all the earth (emphasis added).

For some of us, this way of thinking is hard to understand. But the message is clear: the motive is love and the goal is worship.

To be sure, it is not our duty to bring others to shame. Instead, as the psalmist pleads, it is the Lord who will "fill their faces with shame." We often use shame as a weapon to destroy or tear down. Yet the Lord knows how to use it for the sake of his name and to draw people to himself. This psalm invites us to bring our hearts in accord with God's will while recognizing that he is the one who accomplishes his purpose. C. John Collins comments:

The ultimate reason for Israel's existence is to serve God's purpose of restoring true worship and authentic human life among all mankind; therefore, it is really for the good of these hostile Gentiles that they fail in their plan to 'wipe out Israel' (83:4). The genuine dependence on God expressed in this prayer is thus both devotion to God and goodwill to all mankind.[34]

Parting Reflection

Have you ever seen shame used to bring about obedience? If so, in what ways? How might it be a helpful tool? In what ways might it be harmful?

Parting Prayer

God, we confess that we often stray from you. We are grateful that you love us enough to do what it takes to bring us back to yourself. While we want to despise the shame that comes from the world as you did, Jesus, let us not despise the shame that comes from you directly. Lord, help us to sense and recognize your discipline so that we may seek your face and know that you alone are the Most High over all the earth.

---

34. C. John Collins contributes to the ESV Study Bible by providing the study notes for the Psalms. This quote comes from his commentary there on Psalm 83:9–18. *The ESV Study Bible, English Standard Version* (Wheaton, IL: Crossway Books, 2008).

Taking Others to Court

——————— ·⫶⫶⫶· ———————

What your eyes have seen do not hastily bring into court; for what will you do in the end, when your neighbor puts you to shame? Argue your case with your neighbor directly, and do not disclose another's secret; or else someone who hears you will bring shame upon you, and your ill repute will have no end.

—PROV. 25:8–10

Americans are quick to insist on their rights and sue anyone who challenges them. By contrast, for many East Asians, taking others to court is "regarded as shameful and immoral conduct—where you have the potential of losing 'face' or making your opponent lose significant *mianzi* [face]."[35] According to Proverbs, there's wisdom in handling things outside of court. Even if we win the case, we could lose relationships and our reputation.

First, consider what it means when we've reached the point of hiring lawyers to argue our case against someone else. It might suggest that we've not demonstrated enough patience. Perhaps we've not fostered a relationship or earned the respect that would incline another person to resolve the problem outside of court. Second, if we're hasty to press legal action, what are the potential consequences for both of us? Aside from financial expenses, what damage might a lawsuit do to either party's reputation? That cost might be more than it's worth.

Proverbs 25:9 also mentions a related circumstance. In handling a dispute, one is wise to speak "with your neighbor directly, and do not disclose another's secret." Why? First, misunderstandings might lie beneath the conflict, and

---

35. Haihua Zhang and Geoffrey Baker, *Think Like Chinese* (Alexandria NSW, Australia: Federation Press, 2008), 136. The translation of *mianzi* to "face" is my addition.

making arguments in public often entrenches people into their positions and complicates the resolution process.

Next, people sometimes choose to take disputes not to a law court but to the court of public opinion. They do this by engaging in gossip in its various subtle forms. We might reveal sensitive information or so-called "facts," which are little more than opinions or impressions. A person can easily begin to disparage the accused offender personally. Such people hardly realize how this impacts their reputation. Friends and neighbors soon perceive our character, asking about us, "Are they petty gossips?" or "Do they speak about me like this when I'm not around?"

How we speak of people who offend or hurt us can have lasting effects on our reputations. Are people refreshed by our gracious attitude? Or are they wary to be around us, perhaps unable to trust our intentions? As clergyman Joseph Hall (1574–1656) warns, "A reputation once broken may possibly be repaired, but the world will always keep their eyes on the spot where the crack was."

Parting Reflection

When someone upsets you, are you more likely to go to them in private or tear them down in the eyes of others? How might you improve the way you resolve conflict?

Parting Prayer

Thank you, Father, for such practical wisdom, which both exposes our flaws and foolishness while showing us a better way forward. Spirit, convict us so that we might first bring our concerns to you who knows our hearts.

Honoring a Fool

———— ·il|||ı· ————

Like snow in summer or rain in harvest, so honor is not fitting for a fool.

—PROV. 26:1

Since Arizona has four deserts, much of the state is dry and hot, which is why our first trip to the Grand Canyon surprised us. My family looked forward to seeing the scorched red and orange rock walls that form this natural wonder. Unfortunately, a freak snowstorm forged through the ravine, and we couldn't see more than a few feet past the canyon's ledge. Instead of marveling at true beauty, we missed out on the grandeur of the Grand Canyon and resorted to building a snowman and having snowball fights.

Similarly, and perhaps more striking, is that we've come to expect fools to receive fame and public honor. Media personalities, athletes, politicians, and others often win public acclaim precisely because they are quick to quarrel, express anger, and delight only in sharing their personal opinions. Yet, the Bible calls these people "fools" (Prov. 12:16; 18:2; 20:3).

What happens when we lavish attention on such figures? They believe the hype, thinking themselves to be more intelligent, more skilled, or simply better than others. Proverbs again cautions, "Do you see persons wise in their own eyes? There is more hope for fools than for them" (Prov. 26:12). To be sure, we too can become such fools.

Not only do fools put themselves in danger so also does the person who honors the fool. Proverbs 26:8 says, "It is like binding a stone in a sling to give honor to a fool." The writer describes a careless fighter who harms himself when the stone projects back at him. Examples abound. The manager who promotes a slack worker endangers his own livelihood. Parents who reward or heap hollow praise on a child, simply to boost her self-esteem, will grieve when she continues to make even worse life decisions (1 Sam. 2:29). And what disaster awaits the church who hires a professionally polished but profane pastor (1 Tim. 3:1–7)?

Honor blinds the fool and those who praise him, much like a snowstorm obscured for us both the beauty of the Grand Canyon and the peril of crossing its ledge. However, a new reality will emerge when Christ restores creation: "A fool will no longer be called noble, nor a villain said to be honorable" (Isa. 32:5).

Parting Reflection

How do you honor fools? How have you been honored when you've acted foolishly? Name three people in your life who rarely receive the honor they deserve.

Parting Prayer

Father, we confess that we've acted like fools. In doing so, we endanger both others and ourselves. Thank you for the grace that rescues us from countless poor decisions. Spirit, grant us wisdom to bring you honor and love your people well.

The Proverbs 31 Woman

Charm is deceitful, and beauty is vain, but a woman who fears the Lord is to be praised.

—PROV. 31:30

Many women shake their heads at the thought of living up to the standards of the Proverbs 31 woman. As Adrien Segal notes:

> Not everyone has good business sense or opportunities. Many do not have the gifts and creativity to make clothes for the family and household. I don't know if I've met anyone who is *both a morning person and a night person* like this woman.[36]

And to make matters worse, some in Christian circles tend to idealize this woman, holding her up as the gold standard. This unfortunately leads to unrealistic expectations and the thought that productivity is paramount. Attempting to fully live up to this benchmark leaves us feeling ashamed as we inevitably fall short. However, two points provide clarity about what truly makes the Proverbs 31 woman honorable.

First, most English versions of the Bible translate all the verbs throughout chapter 31 in the present tense. However, in Hebrew, the verbs are all in the past tense. This means that the Proverbs 31 woman had a lifetime to accomplish all these things. She doesn't do it all every day. This understanding should mitigate against unrealistic expectations in the present. Unmet expectations

---

36. Adrien Segal, *Who Can Find Her? Rethinking the Proverbs 31 Standard.* Retrieved from: https://www.desiringgod.org/articles/who-can-find-her.

foster feelings of shame. This reading also emphasizes honoring God in the whole of one's life, not on being as productive as possible.[37]

Second, we need a fresh lens to best understand and apply the Proverbs 31 woman. While it may be true that she's an idealized character, so too are the truly loving person of 1 Corinthians 13:4–8 and the Spirit-filled ideal of Galatians 5:22–23. Tim Keller notes that we must read these passages with the gospel in full view. He says that "those saved by grace in Christ love these texts as guides to pleasing and resembling the one who saved us. The gospel produces people who are eager to obey these patterns and not be crushed by them."[38] We shouldn't be ashamed when we fail to meet these standards because we know that our honor doesn't depend on it. Similarly, our outward appearances and productivity don't determine our true identity. Instead, our honor and identity come from Christ. And a proper response to God's grace is to fear the Lord, striving to honor him in all that we do across a lifetime, just like the Proverbs 31 woman.

Parting Reflection

How have you previously understood the Proverbs 31 woman? In light of these perspectives, does following the Proverbs 31 woman's example seem more attainable?

Parting Prayer

Lord, thank you for not measuring our worth based on our productivity or accomplishments. We praise you that while we still were sinners you died for us. Give us hearts that long to bring honor to your name.

---

37. For further explanation of the concepts in this paragraph, see: https://jasonderouchie.com/wp-content/uploads/2014/09/OTPP20.3-Proverbs.Pt3-DeRouchie.pdf.

38. Timothy Keller, *God's Wisdom for Navigating Life: A Year of Daily Devotions in the Book of Proverbs.* (New York: Viking, 2017), 258.

The Value and Vanity of a Name

—⫻—

The people of long ago are not remembered, nor will there be any remembrance of people yet to come by those who come after them.

—ECCLES. 1:11

Kids often dream of having at least 15 minutes of fame. Such duration now sounds like an eternity. In our age of social media, at best we can wish for 15 *seconds* of fame (and hopefully not infamy). Rather than becoming an astronaut or lawyer, surveys show that nearly one-third of American kids want to be "YouTube famous."[39] Curating one's personal "brand" is seen as the pathway to wealth and happiness. How a small glimmer of truth misleads us into a haze of falsehood!

Ecclesiastes offers sobering insight, noting that the world offers us more futility than fairytales. It's in this reality check that we find wisdom. The vision for life in Ecclesiastes contrasts the delusional ambitions for fame that mark our age. Yet, it offers a balanced perspective that's rooted in the real world. On the one hand, the writer acknowledges the value of a name, "A good name is better than precious ointment, and the day of death, than the day of birth" (Eccles. 7:1). Proverbs 22:1 agrees, "A good name is to be chosen rather than great riches, and favor is better than silver or gold." Our reputations precede us. They open and shut doors of opportunity.

On the other hand, no one will remember most of us in just a few generations. Few people know anything about their own first or second great-grandparents, much less their names. Ecclesiastes shows the vanity of a name, "The people of long ago are not remembered, nor will there be any remembrance

---

39. Paige Leskin, "American kids want to be famous on YouTube, and kids in China want to go to space: survey," *Business Insider,* July 17, 2019. Accessed September 13, 2021, https://www.businessinsider.com/american-kids-youtube-star-astronauts-survey-2019-7.

of people yet to come by those who come after them" (Eccles. 1:11; cf. 9:5). Neither glorious achievement (2:9–11) nor profound wisdom (2:16; 9:15–16) can prevent this inevitable slide into anonymity.

Why then are we constantly allured by the deceptive promises of fame? In part, we confuse being known and praised with being loved. Yet, something else may lurk deeper within our hearts. For some, the desire for celebrity is a grasping for eternity. We begin to think we'll be immortalized if only others remember our names. If we're not forgotten, it's as if we'll live forever; social media fame becomes a virtual form of eternal life. When it comes to reputation, wisdom discerns value from mere vanity.

Parting Reflection

Ecclesiastes offers a balanced view about having a good reputation. How might you need to adjust your perspective when it comes to your reputation? Does a concern for reputation impact the way you use social media?

Parting Prayer

Agreeing with Isaiah 26:8, we pray, "In the path of your judgments, O Lord, we wait for you; your name and your renown are the soul's desire." May we have the wisdom to discern the desire of our hearts. Free us to make you known among all peoples.

God's Supreme Honor and Our Shame

———— ⑅ ————

The haughtiness of people shall be humbled, and the pride of everyone
shall be brought low; and the Lord alone will be exalted on that day.

—ISA. 2:17

The second chapter of Isaiah introduces The Day of the Lord. This term typically refers to a time when God judges the world and fulfills his purposes at
the end of time. But what will be judged?

As the above verse states, "The Lord alone will be exalted on that day."
Later in Isaiah, God says, "I am the Lord, that is my name; my glory I give
to no other" (42:8). In the next chapter, he says that everything was created
for his glory (43:6-7). Elsewhere, God's people are called to "declare his glory
among the nations" (Ps. 96:3). As believers, we are called to do all things for
God's glory (1 Cor. 10:31). In short, God alone is worthy of supreme honor,
and humans were created to live in a way that honors God with all of our
hearts and displays his glory to the watching world.

So, again, what will be judged on The Day of the Lord? Isaiah 2 indicts
the Israelites on three charges. First, they are idolaters (2:6, 8). Second, they
are greedy (2:7). Third, and most emphasized, is that they exalt themselves
(2:11-17). When we exalt ourselves over and against God, it will end in our
shame: "For the Lord of hosts has a day against all that is proud and lofty,
against all that is lifted up—and it shall be brought low" (Isa. 2:12 ESV).
Revelation 19:11-21 vividly describes The Day of the Lord. A paraphrase
of these events says, "Those united against God's Messiah are reduced to
slain corpses unworthy of human burial. Wild birds gorge themselves on
their rotting flesh, a symbol of utter desecration and disgrace."[40] Thus, God's

---

40. Jayson Georges and Mark Baker, *Ministering in Honor-Shame Cultures: Biblical Founda-*
tions and Practical Essentials (Downers Grove, IL: IVP, 2016), 89.

judgment on The Day of the Lord will bring shame and humiliation to those who exalt themselves. Sadly, we are all culpable of these charges. Yet, we are not without hope.

Commenting on Isaiah 2, Andrew Shanks summarizes: "Our shame runs so deep that the only hope of overcoming it is a glory that runs even deeper."[41] And such glory has come in Jesus Christ, who is "the radiance of the glory of God and the exact imprint of his nature" (Heb. 1:3). Praise God for sending his Son to overcome our shame so that we may be with him in his glory for eternity.

Parting Reflection

Have you ever considered God's supreme honor as the foundation of his judgment against humanity? Why does it matter if we dishonor God? Why does exalting ourselves offend God?

Parting Prayer

God, we recognize that you alone are worthy. We confess that we often exalt ourselves, not recognizing your hand in all that we have. Jesus, thank you for redeeming us. Spirit, help us to truthfully say about you, "For from him and through him and to him are all things. To him be glory forever. Amen" (Rom. 11:36).

---

41. Andrew Shanks is the Lead Pastor at The Little Church in the Vale in Gates Mills, Ohio. The quote is taken from a sermon titled, *A Deeper Glory* on May 5, 2019, http://little.church /about/sermon-archive-2/isaiah/.

The Curse Reversed

The wilderness and the dry land shall be glad, the desert shall rejoice and blossom; like the crocus it shall blossom abundantly, and rejoice with joy and singing.

—ISA. 35:1–2

One result of the Fall is that the ground does not bear fruit as it was designed. In Genesis 3:17–19, God curses the ground. Since then, humans have brought forth food only through burdensome toil. That said, work is not the curse itself. After all, God gave Adam and Eve jobs to do before the Fall. But there is a stark contrast between the abundantly fruitful land in Eden and the cursed circumstances by which we now acquire food: "In toil you shall eat of it all the days of your life; thorns and thistles it shall bring forth for you" (Gen. 3:17–18).

Isaiah no doubt had this curse on the ground in mind when he wrote 35:1–2 (quoted above). To this day, Isaiah's prophecy remains unfulfilled. The curse has not yet been lifted; however, the assurance that it will remains. The apostle Paul alludes to Genesis 3:17–19 when he writes:

> *For the creation was subjected to futility, not of its own will but by the will of the one who subjected it, in hope that the creation itself will be set free from its bondage to decay and will obtain the freedom of the glory of the children of God.*
> —Rom. 8:20–21

In other words, the curse on the ground *will be* reversed. In some sense, the ground (i.e., creation) will have its status changed from one of shame to one of honor.

Furthermore, Paul ties together this state of reversal with the fortunes of humanity. Along with the world, the human family will be restored to the Creator God. After all, Adam and Eve were sent out of the Garden and away from the unencumbered presence of God. Apart from Christ, this is the dreadful state of reality that we all find ourselves in. Yet, the Lord tells us through Isaiah and Paul that this is not the end of the matter. Through Christ, broken humanity will again be made whole, and God will bring exiled people from every tribe, tongue, and nation back home. The curse will be reversed for both the ground and humanity.

Parting Reflection

None of us have ever seen the earth as God originally created it. That being the case, why do you think it matters that God will reverse the curse on the ground? What would it mean if God's redemptive work did not reach all aspects of the curse?

Parting Prayer

God, because of the great love with which you loved us, you sent your Son to reverse the curse and to reconcile us to yourself. For this, we praise you. And not us only, but also the whole of your creation magnifies your praise. We know that these realities are "already, but not yet." Help us to anchor our hope in the assurance that you will do all you have promised.

Status Reversal

Every valley shall be lifted up, and every mountain and hill be made low; the uneven ground shall become level, and the rough places a plain.

—ISA. 40:4

When a person gives allegiance to Christ and is saved, their world turns upside down. The believer passes from death to life, from blindness to having sight. They are transferred from the domain of darkness into Christ's kingdom. Those who were enemies of God are reconciled to him. They now live by the Spirit, not the flesh. The term *status reversal* succinctly sums up these changes.

The Bible is filled with instances of such status reversals. Among them is the reality that God removes our shame and restores our honor. This movement from shame to honor is practical. Consider how often God caused a barren woman to bear a child. Such women include Sarah, Rebekah, Rachel, Hannah, and Elizabeth. In ancient Near-Eastern culture (and in many contemporary cultures), barrenness gives birth to a great sense of shame. Undoubtedly, when God miraculously allowed these women to conceive, they tangibly felt the removal of their shame. Elizabeth sums up her feelings, "This is what the Lord has done for me when he looked favorably on me and took away the disgrace I have endured among my people" (Luke 1:25).

Also, Mary, the mother of Jesus, experienced her own status reversal. Initially, a young woman betrothed to Joseph, an angel told her that she was pregnant before marriage. This would have unquestionably become a source of shame for her within the community. Several months later, Mary comes to understand the surpassing honor that was to be hers through this pregnancy. She proclaims in the Magnificat, "My soul magnifies the Lord, and my spirit rejoices in God my Savior, for he has looked with favor on the lowliness of his servant. Surely, from now on all generations will call me blessed" (Luke 1:46–48).

God still lifts up the lowly and levels those who have a lofty status. Christ changes our character, upending our worldly sense of honor and shame. Previously outsiders, we now belong to a new community made up of the adopted children of God.

Parting Reflection

Think back on your life. What elements of your life has the Lord reversed, as though bringing honor from shame?

Parting Prayer

Lord, we thank you that you are the God who changes our circumstances. You don't merely change our legal status, as though you were a distant judge. Rather, you intervene in our lives personally in such a way that you remove our shame and give us honor. We long to be in eternity with you, where we will dwell with you in glory.

Honored through Shame

―――――――――― ·╢╟· ――――――――――

*He had no form or majesty that we should look at him, nothing in his
appearance that we should desire him. He was despised and rejected
by others; a man of suffering and acquainted with infirmity; and as
one from whom others hide their faces he was despised, and we held
him of no account.*

—ISA. 53:2–3

Authors in the New Testament loved Isaiah 52:13–53:12. They draw from
these chapters more than almost any other Old Testament text. The prophet
sounds almost cryptic at times, and his words confuse many readers. Yet, early
Christians saw in this passage a foreshadowing of Christ. Isaiah ironically
speaks of a righteous servant who suffers shame, even death, according to
God's will. Somehow this travesty of justice removes *our* iniquity!

We learn many things about the righteous servant in this passage. First,
God says he will be exalted and astonish the kings of the earth (53:13–15). Still,
there is nothing magnificent about this servant's appearance, and he will be
despised and rejected (53:2–3). In traditional honor-shame cultures, a person
must retaliate when someone impugns their honor. Not defending oneself is
shameful. It's as if the insulted person implicitly agrees with their opponent.
But what does the servant do? "He did not open his mouth; like a lamb that
is led to the slaughter" (53:7). The silence only compounds his shame before
a watching public. Isaiah 53:12 underscores a critical point:

*I will allot him a portion with the great, and he shall divide the spoil with
the strong; because he poured out himself to death, and was numbered with
the transgressors; yet he bore the sin of many, and made intercession for the
transgressors.*

In short, God's servant is honored *through* shame. The servant finds satisfaction when the Lord's will prospers through him, making many righteous (53:10–11). To our surprise, we too are honored through his shame. By suffering disgrace, Christ takes away our sin, grief, and sorrows (53:4, 11, 12). Although "we esteemed him stricken, smitten by God, and afflicted," his humiliation brings us peace and heals our wounds (53:4–5).

Christ's ministry becomes a paradigm forcing us to rethink what is honorable and what is shameful. Along with New Testament writers, the servant from Isaiah challenges us to reimagine how God's people, like Christ, might be honored through shame.

Parting Reflection

The people who persecuted Jesus did not understand the true nature of glory. Their expectations led them astray. How might you miss out on true honor because you accept a worldly understanding of what is shameful?

Parting Prayer

How majestic are you, Jesus, who humbled yourself and experienced shame at the hands of sinners. Your sovereignty and wisdom are matchless. We admit how often we think public accolades indicate worth. We rest content in your divine plan to bring us honor even if through shame.

When Feeling Ashamed
Is Not a Bad Thing

———— ·ıɪɪɪ· ————

Look up to the bare heights, and see! Where have you not been lain with? By the waysides you have sat waiting for lovers, like a nomad in the wilderness. You have polluted the land with your whoring and wickedness. Therefore the showers have been withheld, and the spring rain has not come; yet you have the forehead of a whore, you refuse to be ashamed.

—JER. 3:2–3

I (Ryan) lived a lifestyle full of debauchery while a sophomore in college. The strange thing about it is that I knew it. Having been raised going to church every Sunday, I had a general idea of how God wanted me to live. Yet, I knew I was far off the path. As the Lord sought me that spring semester, there were a couple of instances where I began to draw near to Christ but then withdrew, returning to my sinful lifestyle. In short, I was aware of my shameful behavior, but I wasn't ready to face it or give it up.

We often think that feeling ashamed is inherently a bad thing and speak of it in a predominantly negative tone. Naturally, this can spill over into our spiritual thinking as well. As Hailey Bieber, a professing Christian, once said, "I believe a relationship with God is the opposite of feeling shame. I don't think that God wants you to feel shameful and that everything is a bad thing."[42] Is she right? Does God not want us to feel ashamed?

---

42. David Artavia, "Hailey Bieber says it was 'extremely difficult' navigating Justin's sobriety after having witnessed her dad's drug addiction." *Yahoo! life*, November 10, 2021, https://www.yahoo.com/lifestyle/hailey-bieber-difficult-navigating-justin-sobriety-dad-drug-addiction-175445779.html.

Yes and no. Yes, it is correct that in Christ all of our shame is taken away (1 Pet. 2:6). However, there is an "already but not yet" aspect to this removal of shame. In this life, shame is still present, and it has its purpose. Bieber is wrong that God doesn't want us to feel ashamed if we are acting in violation of his revealed will. He doesn't ignore our sins or tell us that it's okay. Instead, he calls us to feel ashamed of our sin before him. This can be seen in the passage quoted above.

In Jeremiah 3, God rather sharply rebukes the Israelites for their vile behavior. Even worse than the depth of their depravity is that they won't own up to it before God. Of course, their sin is a big problem. But compounding the issue is that they "refuse to be ashamed" (Jer. 3:3).

In many respects, this is where I was back in college. I knew my behavior was wrong, but I wasn't ready to own up to it before God. Yet, one morning he brought me to the end of myself. At that moment, I felt unworthy and deeply ashamed before God, like the tax collector who "would not even lift up his eyes to heaven, but beat his breast and saying, 'God, be merciful to me, a sinner!'" (Luke 18:13). When we refuse to feel ashamed of our sin before God, we distance ourselves from him. Thus, feeling ashamed is not always a bad thing, especially when it brings us to the cross.

Parting Reflection

Hiding our shame only produces spiritual death (Rom. 6:20–21). Is there any area of your life about which you feel ashamed before God? Is it a result of sin on your part? If so, bring it to him now and let him cleanse you.

Parting Prayer

Jesus, thank you that through your death on the cross, we are clothed in robes of righteousness. Spirit, help us to not be obstinate with our sin. Convict us concerning sin and lead us to the cross.

Apart from Christ, Our Destiny Is Shame

———— ⑈ ————

This is your lot, the portion I have measured out to you, says the Lord, because you have forgotten me and trusted in lies. I myself will lift up your skirts over your face, and your shame will be seen.

—JER. 13:25–26

Jeremiah 13 begins with God instructing the prophet to purchase a loincloth and then bury it in a rocky place, where it will inevitably become ruined. This act symbolizes Judah's great pride, which clings to them like a loincloth and ruins them. As a result of Judah's pride and idolatry, exile is threatened: "The towns of the Negeb are shut up with no one to open them; all Judah is taken into exile, wholly taken into exile" (13:19).

God foresees Judah's objection to this condemnation. He answers, "And if you say in your heart, 'Why have these things come upon me?' it is for the greatness of your iniquity that your skirts are lifted up, and you suffer violence" (13:22). Judah will not suffer innocently. God will ensure that their life of pride results in humiliation. It is the Lord who will "lift up their skirts" in order to expose their disgrace. These words show that judgment for sin goes beyond a legal sentence and includes tangible shame.

A nearly identical condemnation is seen elsewhere, "I am against you, says the Lord of hosts, and will lift up your skirts over your face; and I will let nations look on your nakedness and kingdoms on your shame" (Nah. 3:5). The nation that was once viewed as honorable and respected by those surrounding it is now destined for shame and disrepute if they continue to reject the Lord. Similarly, we dishonor God with our sinfulness, and our shame will one day be exposed. The reputable life that we have built for ourselves will come crashing down.

Yet, this is not the end of the story. Jeremiah prophesies about the coming righteous Branch (Jer. 23:5–6; 33:14–16), promising that he will "restore [Judah's] fortunes, and will have mercy upon them" (Jer. 33:26). Centuries later, this righteous Branch, Jesus, came to reconcile to God those who would believe in him:

> *Indeed, God did not send the Son into the world to condemn the world, but in*
> *order that the world might be saved through him. Those who believe in him are*
> *not condemned; but those who do not believe are condemned already, because*
> *they have not believed in the name of the only Son of God.*
> —John 3:17–18

If we pridefully assume that our heritage or involvement in Christian activities will save us, we too will be condemned, and our disgrace will be exposed. Indeed, apart from Christ, our destiny is shame.

Parting Reflection

Have you ever considered that judgment for sin could involve tangible shame? Can you think of an example of a person's sin that led them to fall into disrepute? Has your sin ever brought humiliation to you?

Parting Prayer

Lord, we confess that we have acted pridefully toward you. Without Christ, we are "condemned already" because of sin. Father, thank you for sending your Son to save us. Jesus, thank you for your life, death, and resurrection for us. Spirit, help us to rejoice in your salvation.

God's Face Against Us

―――――――――― ⫶⫶⫶ ――――――――――

Behold, I will set my face against you for harm, to cut off all Judah.

—JER. 44:11 ESV

The concept of "face" is complex and with many layers of meaning. In many cultures, one's face is bound up in how well they measure up to their role in society. An individual can lose face for failing to "maintain one's social status, to function adequately in a given role, or to safeguard integrity of character in one's general conduct."[43] If someone fails to meet their societal responsibilities, others can take actions that cause that person to lose face. The same ideas are seen clearly throughout Scripture:

> *For I have set my face against this city for harm and not for good, declares the Lord; it shall be given into the hand of the king of Babylon, and he shall burn it with fire"*
> —Jer. 21:10 ESV

> *I will set my face against them; I will make them a sign and a byword and cut them off from the midst of my people; and you shall know that I am the Lord.*
> —Ezek. 14:8[44]

In both passages, the concept of face does not simply seem to mean that God is either present or not. Instead, they speak of God's face being against someone. And when God sets his face against someone, he has an active disposition to bring shame to that person. So, how do people invite God to turn his face against them? Again, let's turn to the Bible:

---

43. David Yau-fai Ho, "On the Concept of Face," 872.
44. For further meditation, see Jeremiah 33:5 and Ezekiel 15:7–8.

The face of the Lord is against all evildoers, to cut off the remembrance of them from the earth"
—Ps. 34:16

And many nations will pass by this city, and all of them will say one to another, "Why has the Lord dealt in this way with that great city?" And they will answer, "Because they abandoned the covenant of the Lord their God, and worshiped other gods and served them.
—Jer. 22:8–9

In the Old Testament, God's people repeatedly fail to meet their covenantal responsibilities to God and one another. Therefore, God turns his face against them. Again, this does not mean that God simply withdraws his presence from them. Beyond that, the Lord acts to cause them to lose face. As noted in a previous entry, one purpose of parental shaming is to teach children to obey. So also, God's active disposition against them is not only to induce shame but also to bring them into obedience. May these passages remind us of our covenant responsibility to one another and God's fatherly love for us.

Parting Reflection

Do you think that God still turns his face away from his children today? Why do you say this? How might God use shame as a way of disciplining, not punishing, us?

Parting Prayer

Father, you alone are holy. We praise you for your infinite faithfulness to your covenant. We confess that we so often fail on our end. Thank you for loving us so much that you actively grab our attention in order to bring us into obedience.

Saved from, Through, and for Shame

———— ⑃ ————

I will establish my covenant with you, and you shall know that I am
the Lord, in order that you may remember and be confounded, and
never open your mouth again because of your shame, when I forgive
you all that you have done, says the Lord God.

—EZEK. 16:62–63

Jesus saves us from shame, right? Yes and no. While it can certainly be destructive, the Bible has a more nuanced view on shame. For example, Ezekiel relates shame and salvation in three ways. First, God's people are saved *from* shame. God expressly states that he hid his face from Israel because of their "uncleanness and transgressions," which resulted in their disgraced state of being exiled (Ezek. 39:22–24). Immediately following, God speaks of mercy toward Israel. Out of concern for his name, he will no longer hide his face from them and will "restore the fortunes of Jacob." As a result, God says that Israel "shall forget their shame all the treachery they have practiced against me." Deliverance from shame brings restored honor (Ezek. 39:25–29).

Second, God's people are saved *through* shame. Shame is a part of the process whereby God achieves our salvation. God commands Ezekiel, "Describe the temple to the house of Israel, and let them measure the pattern; and let them be ashamed of their iniquities. When they are ashamed of all that they have done, make known to them the plan of the temple" (Ezek. 43:10–11). The prophet gives a vision for when God's glory returns and fills the temple. His message intends to evoke shame. In this sense, shame precedes reconciliation in the same way that guilt precedes forgiveness.

Third, God's people are saved *for* shame. God's salvation brings a new perspective on what is honorable and praiseworthy. The prophet says, "I will restore your own fortunes in their midst, that you may bear your disgrace and be ashamed of all that you have done, becoming a consolation to them" (Ezek. 16:53–54 ESV). Israel's restoration should instill a proper sense of shame that leads God's people to no longer be indifferent or boastful of their ways (Ezek. 16:59–63).

Those who rebel against the Lord are shameless, unable to discern right and wrong (Jer. 3:3; 6:15). In a sense, full reconciliation depends on repentance and gaining a new heart (Ezek. 36:26–27). Our ambition is not to eliminate shame but to gain the right kind of shame. After all, we are saved *from*, *through*, and *for* shame.

Parting Reflection

Can you recall a time that you felt a proper sense of shame because you recognized some wrong you had done? When has a healthy sense of shame guarded you against making ungodly or unwise decisions?

Parting Prayer

Lord, you are the God who can even use shame for our salvation. How amazing! We pray for you to grant us supernatural wisdom to discern what is truly honorable and genuinely shameful. You can do more than we can ever imagine!

God's Face is Eternally for Us

––––––––––––––––– ·⫷|||⫸· –––––––––––––––––

And I will never again hide my face from them, when I pour out my
spirit upon the house of Israel, says the Lord God.

—EZEK. 39:29

It sure sounds nice to believe that God's face is eternally for us and not against us. Likewise, it is wonderful to know that nothing can separate us from the love of God in Christ Jesus (Rom. 8:35–39). But how can we be certain that these realities are true for us?

Paul bookends Romans 8 with two truths. First, there is no condemnation for those who are in Christ. Second, nothing can separate a believer from the love of God. In the verses between them, Paul makes several arguments to demonstrate the veracity of those truths. In 8:31–32, he forcefully argues from the greater to the lesser. He presents two events—God not sparing his own Son and God giving us all things. Paul says that since God already did the harder thing (not sparing his own Son), then, of course, he will do what is easier (graciously give us all things). We then can place our faith in this rock-solid truth, trusting that God is eternally for us.

Paul makes a second argument, this time concerning the giving of the Holy Spirit. He states that everyone who is in Christ has the Spirit. If one does not have the Spirit, then they are not in Christ. The apostle connects the giving of the Spirit to God's being for us, assuring us that we are God's children. The Spirit empowers us to live out our faith in righteousness and prayer.

In Ezekiel 39, God makes a surprising connection between his face being for the house of Israel and the giving of the Holy Spirit. The verse quoted above says that once God pours out his Spirit upon them, he will no longer hide his face from them. God will indeed have an active disposition of working for their good, which is demonstrated by the giving of the Spirit. Believers today, whether ethnic Jews or Gentiles, are a part of "spiritual Israel" and can be certain that this promise holds for us too. Elsewhere, Paul says that God has given us his Spirit as a guarantee, or down payment, of our eternal hope (2 Cor. 1:22). We can rest assured that God's face is toward us now because he has given us his Spirit to help, teach, convict, and magnify Christ in our hearts.

Parting Reflection

In honor-shame cultures, what does it mean to give someone face? Do you think God gives us face by granting us the Holy Spirit? If so, in what ways?

Parting Prayer

Lord, thank you for the incomprehensible gift of your Spirit living in us. We confess that far too often we try to do things on our own. To set the mind on the flesh is death, but to set the mind on the Spirit is life and peace. Lord, we know that through Christ your face is indeed toward us. So, help us not to quench your Spirit.

We Have Sinned and Done Wrong

———————— ⫴ ————————

*I prayed to the Lord my God and made confession, saying, "Ah, Lord,
great and awesome God, keeping covenant and steadfast love with
those who love you and keep your commandments, we have sinned
and done wrong, acted wickedly and rebelled, turning aside from your
commandments and ordinances . . . Righteousness is on your side, O
Lord, but open shame, as at this day, falls on us."*

—DAN. 9:4–7

Daniel shows remarkable faithfulness to God. At a young age, he is taken
as an exile to Babylon. Under great pressure, Daniel refuses to forget God
and embrace Babylonian culture with all of its idolatry. God blesses Daniel
and gives him favor before the Babylonian leaders, allowing him to interpret
Nebuchadnezzar's dream. This leads to Daniel being promoted within the
Babylonian court. Many years later, he refuses to stop worshiping God despite
an edict from Darius. Daniel is thrown into a lion's den, but God protects
him. Given all this, it seems remarkable that when Daniel offers a prayer to
God for Israel, he includes himself as one who has "sinned and done wrong,
acted wickedly and rebelled" (Dan. 9:5).

A similar scene is found in Ezra 9. During the reign of Artaxerxes king
of Persia, God raises up Ezra and sends him to teach the Israelites who had
returned to the holy land. He is described as having favor from God, "For the
hand of the Lord his God was upon him" (Ezra 7:6). Also, he is a priest in the
line of Aaron and is skilled as a scribe of God's law. Shortly after arriving, Ezra
learns of the rampant idolatry and faithlessness of the returned exiles. Similar
to Daniel, he offers up a prayer for Israel: "O my God, I am too ashamed and
embarrassed to lift my face to you, my God, for our iniquities have risen higher
than our heads, and our guilt has mounted up to the heavens" (Ezra 9:6). Ezra,
like Daniel, was faithful to the Lord and did not commit these acts of idolatry
and faithlessness. So why do they lump themselves in with everyone else?

Undoubtedly, a primary driver is their orientation within an honor-shame culture. In such cultures, the group is valued over the individual. It follows that people are not viewed as unconnected entities, but rather, individuals are inseparably linked to the larger group. Instead of each person being independent of one another, they are *inter*dependent.

So, when Daniel and Ezra witnessed the iniquity of the Israelites, they didn't think to disassociate themselves from the group. It wasn't "those people" who sinned. Instead, Daniel and Ezra themselves felt the shame and guilt of Israel and thus instinctively included themselves as they confessed sin and lamented to God.

Parting Reflection

When you see the sin of other Christians, how do you respond? How might an entire community share in the guilt of specific individuals who do wrong?

Parting Prayer

Father, we praise you for bringing us into a community of believers. As David says in Psalm 16:3, "As for the saints of the land, they are the excellent ones, in whom is all my delight" (ESV). Spirit, help us to love our brothers and sisters in Christ. Even though it may be messy, help us to see the beauty of community.

The Other Side of Status Reversal

———————— ·⫴⫴⫴· ————————

The more they increased, the more they sinned against me; I will change their glory into shame.

—HOSEA 4:7 ESV

In previous entries, we saw how one of God's modes of operation is to reverse one's status from shame to honor. However, the passage quoted above is just one example that the inverse can also be true. In Hosea 4, the Lord hurls accusations at the northern kingdom of Israel, and the priests in particular, for their unfaithfulness. In words that must have shocked the original hearers, God reveals one consequence of their sin: "Therefore the land mourns, and all who live in it languish; together with the wild animals and the birds of the air, even the fish of the sea are perishing" (Hosea 4:3).

These words are shocking because God had promised the Israelites a land flowing with milk and honey (i.e., abundant agricultural fertility). Just before they enter the Promised Land for the first time, God promises blessings for obedience to the people and their land: "Blessed shall be the fruit of your womb, the fruit of your ground, and the fruit of your livestock, both the increase of your cattle and the issue of your flock. Blessed shall be your basket and your kneading bowl" (Deut. 28:4–5). However, moments later, Moses warns the people of what disobedience could bring, "But if you will not obey the Lord your God diligently . . . Cursed shall be your basket and your kneading bowl. Cursed shall be the fruit of your womb and the fruit of your ground" (Deut. 28:15–18).

Despite Moses' warnings, Hosea 4:7 (quoted above) suggests that this group of Israelites were oblivious to the consequences of their disobedience by revealing that the more the people increased in material fruitfulness, "the more they sinned against [God]." As a result, God declares that he will reverse their status from glory to shame.

The book of Hosea is replete with judgments against the Israelites who break God's covenant. The northern kingdom's glory was indeed turned to shame when the Assyrians sacked the region in 722 BC and took the people off into exile. And yet, through it all, God's love for his people prevails. In Hosea 3:5, the prophet says that after the exile "the Israelites shall return and seek the Lord their God, and David their king." Centuries later, the Son of David, the true King, left his place of glory so that he may take our shame in order to raise us up to glory with him.

Parting Reflection

Do you ever feel the temptation to rest on the laurels of your faith? Do you know anyone who might presume upon their status before God based on their cultural background or simply attending church? How can we actively be on guard against these pitfalls?

Parting Prayer

Lord, we confess that you are indeed the founder and perfecter of our faith. Apart from you, we can do nothing. Help us to fight the good fight of faith.

They Will Not Be Put to Shame

———————— ·⫴⫴⫴· ————————

You shall know that I am in the midst of Israel, and that I, the Lord, am your God and there is no other. And my people shall never again be put to shame.

—JOEL 2:27

Israel suffered imaginable pain. In Joel, a horde of locusts decimates crops, leaving people to waste away in hunger. Meanwhile, an invading nation pounces on its weakened prey with lion-like teeth. Israel faces the consequences of its faithlessness. Anguish then spreads faster than the fires that consumed their pastures.

The prophet beckons the priests to prayer, "Spare your people, O Lord, and do not make your heritage a mockery, a byword among the nations. Why should it be said among the peoples, 'Where is their God?'" (Joel 2:17). Unless the Lord relents, the world will forever recount Israel's humiliation, like a proverb passed along through countless generations. In Joel 2, Israel's "shame" refers to more than a psychological mindset; it points to dire circumstances that call into question their relationship with God. Such shame casts doubt on their existence as a people.

Yet, Joel knows that more is at stake than the disgrace of a wayward nation. The Lord's reputation is at stake! God has tied his name with that of his people. The Lord promised to honor Abraham's offspring. And so, he extends an invitation, "Return to me with all your heart, with fasting, with weeping, and with mourning; rend your hearts and not your clothing" (Joel 2:12). When they do, the Lord's response is practical: He sends grain, wine, and oil. He removes their oppressor.

Joel 2:23 adds, "He has given the early rain for your vindication." The word translated "vindication" is elsewhere translated as "justification" or "righteousness." The Lord then twice repeats, "my people shall never again be put to shame" (2:26, 27). In effect, Joel says that since God has justified (i.e., vindicated) them via the early rains, they can have confidence he'll not let them be put to shame in perpetuity, despite their current conditions. A similar line of thinking exists in Romans. Not only does Paul quote Joel 2:32 ("Everyone who calls on the name of the Lord shall be saved") in Romans 10:13. He also links justification with the promise that God will not put his people to shame (Rom. 9:33; 10:11).

The Lord saves us even from self-inflicted shame resulting from sin. Yet, he does more than expunge our disgrace. He vindicates his own name by showing himself faithful to his people. And so, we proclaim, "Surely he has done great things!" (Joel 2:20).

Parting Reflection

Shame is a common result of sin, whether ours or that of others. How has the Lord freed you from your shame and reminded you that you belong to him?

Parting Prayer

Lord, because of our sin, we bring much shame on ourselves and, more grievously, upon your name. We lament not only our condition but also how we've been unfaithful and not loved you well. Restore our joy in you as you fulfill your word of hope and salvation.

I Shall See the Lord's Vindication

———————— ⑈⑈⑈ ————————

He will bring me out to the light; I shall see his vindication. Then my enemy will see, and shame will cover her who said to me, "Where is the Lord your God?"

—MIC. 7:9–10

Some people take peculiar pleasure in seeing public figures fall from prominence. Perhaps their hidden sin is exposed, or they say something deemed offensive. As a result, they are "canceled." Such individuals might deserve public criticism, but it's also possible that there's more to their story than we're aware of.

Micah faces a similar situation, where his enemies rejoice over his troubles. While society seems to collapse in moral chaos around him, he doesn't blame shift as if to excuse his sin. Instead, he confesses, "I must bear the indignation of the Lord, because I have sinned against him" (7:9). This humility also allows the prophet to wait for the Lord, confident that God will save him and bring restoration (7:7-20). What could possibly ground such hope?

Micah knows the Lord will judge on his behalf against his enemies. In this way, the prophet will see God's "vindication" (the word typically translated as "righteousness"). People do not always think of the Lord's judgment or righteousness in such favorable, saving terms. Yet, this hope enables Micah to see beyond the present pain. Verse 10 helps us to make sense of this circumstance. Micah's accusers assume that God either disowns Micah or else is unable to save him. These enemies do not understand the Lord's righteousness. He always keeps his promises. He brings salvation, often through suffering. Injustice and accusation tempt God's people to forsake their hope in him. If only they had Paul's confident assertion that such "hope does not put us to shame" (Rom. 5:5 ESV)!

The Lord makes clear to both Micah and Paul what is the ultimate basis of a person's honor or shame. It is directly tied to one's hope. Who or what is the source of our hope? Will that person or object eventually disappoint us? If so, shame will cover us just as it covers those who doubt the faithfulness of Micah's God (7:18–20). When the Lord pardons iniquity and restores the world to right, "the nations shall see and be ashamed of all their might" (7:16).

Parting Reflection

When have you hoped in something or someone else other than the Lord and his righteous? How did it lead to disappointment and perhaps even shame or embarrassment?

Parting Prayer

We agree with Nehemiah 9:8, "You have fulfilled your promise, for you are righteous." Father, all your promises are yes in Christ. Spirit, make us steadfast in true hope that will never put us to shame.

Whom Does God Call Worthless?

—————— ·⫶⫶⫶· ——————

The Lord has commanded concerning you: "Your name shall be perpet-uated no longer; from the house of your gods I will cut off the carved image and the cast image. I will make your grave, for you are worthless."

—NAH. 1:14

No one wants to be forgotten, for then it seems we had never lived. George Elliot once said, "Our dead are never dead to us, until we have forgotten them." For some, being remembered is a kind of immortality. This concern is evident in various cultural practices. When Chinese women marry, they do not take their husband's surname; instead, they keep their own to perpetuate their family's name. In many cultures, preserving one's name is a primary reason for having children.

Imagine then the severity of the Lord's condemnation of Nineveh, capital of Assyria, when he says, "Your name shall be perpetuated no longer." He even says to the Ninevites, "you are worthless." What spurred such a fierce response from God? A few reasons include Assyria's oppression of God's people (1:12), brutality, and overall godlessness (3:1–5). They persist in their ways because they trust in their false gods (1:14). The Assyrians have little concern to change their ways because they believe their idols will secure them with riches and renown.

This story is not merely about morality. In ancient cultures, one's gods determined one's king, and vice versa. To give allegiance to idols meant rejecting the Lord as king, and we know God does not tolerate such dishonor forever. This background sheds light on Nahum 1:15, where the prophet brings good news for Judah. In fact, the word used in both the Hebrew and Greek Old Testament is "gospel." For ancient listeners, "gospel" was not a "spiritual" word. It referred to a royal announcement, declaring a king's ascension or military victory.

Nahum explains how the Lord, Judah's divine king, upholds his honor by saving his people. "The Lord is restoring the majesty of Jacob, as well as the majesty of Israel" (2:2). He does so by shaming their enemies. God tells Nineveh:

> *I am against you, says the Lord of hosts, and will lift up your skirts over your*
> *face; and I will let nations look on your nakedness and kingdoms on your shame.*
> *I will throw filth at you and treat you with contempt, and make you a spectacle.*
> —Nah. 3:5–6

Similarly, the gospel declares how God raises up Christ as king, putting all his enemies under his feet (1 Cor. 15:24–27). Unlike the Assyrians, Christ's followers will never be put to shame, for, instead of looking to the false promises of idols, we put our trust in God.

Parting Reflection

What are potential idols in your life that promise to perpetuate a name for you (and perhaps your family, church, business, or nation)? How have you unwittingly shown allegiance to these idols?

Parting Prayer

Lord, we know that idols do not determine our worth. You do. We rejoice in the gospel that declares Christ's victory over sin and death. Those who trust in you will not be put to shame!

Should We Be Shameless?

The Lord within it is righteous; he does no wrong; every morning he renders his judgment; each dawn without fail; but the unjust knows no shame.

—ZEPH. 3:5

We often hear people say, "Shame is bad. We need to get rid of it." Is that true? Does eliminating shame mean becoming shameless? No, not according to the Bible. In contemporary and ancient languages, calling someone "shameless" is an insult, not a compliment. It suggests that one has no sense of what is right or wrong. Such individuals lack basic human sensitivity to others.

In Zephaniah 2:1, when the Lord addresses the people, "O shameless nation," he speaks to their stubborn, unteachable hearts. In contrast to the righteous Lord, "the unjust knows no shame" (3:5 quoted above). A proper sense of shame is what we today call a person's "conscience." To be impervious to shame is to have a heart hardened to the effects of sin. This is why Job defends himself to his friends, "These ten times you have cast reproach upon me; *are you not ashamed to wrong me?*" (Job 19:3 emphasis added). In the same way, the Lord says in Jeremiah 6:15, "They acted shamefully, they committed abomination; yet they were not ashamed, they did not know how to blush."[45]

Ironically, the one who is shameless is most shameful in the eyes of God! Observe what he says to Jerusalem in Zephaniah 3:1–2, "Ah, *soiled, defiled, oppressing city!* It has listened to no voice; it has accepted no correction. It has not trusted in the Lord; it has not drawn near to its God" (emphasis added). The Lord then calls their officials "wolves" and their prophets "reckless, faithless persons" (3:3–4). These words highlight the magnitude of their disgraceful behavior. They do not honor the Lord with faith by taking refuge

---

45. In the New Testament, compare Romans 1:27; 1 Peter 5:2; Titus 1:11; Ephesians 5:3, 12.

in him. Therefore, the prophet foretells the coming day when God's people will be sent into exile.

However, Zephaniah does not end here. Shame doesn't have the last word. God works to bring glory from shame, and honor amid humiliation. In Zephaniah 3:18-19, the Lord says:

> *I will remove disaster from you, so that you will not bear reproach for it. I will deal with all your oppressors at that time. And I will save the lame and gather the outcast, and I will change their shame into praise and renown in all the earth.*

Such promises are not for the shameless, but rather for those who "call on the name of the Lord" (Zeph. 3:9).

Parting Reflection

Some Westerners like to say, "I don't care what anyone else thinks," when in fact, they, more than most people, care deeply about others' opinions. But what if they truly meant it? Why might it be dangerous to not care what anyone else thinks?

Parting Prayer

Lord, thank you for giving us a new heart and a new spirit (Ezek. 36:26). Make us more sensitive to your Spirit so that we would honor what is honorable and judge shameful what you regard as shameful.

Subverting Status Symbols

Rejoice greatly, O daughter Zion! Shout aloud, O daughter Jerusalem! Lo, your king comes to you; triumphant and victorious is he, humble and riding on a donkey, on a colt, the foal of a donkey.

—ZECH. 9:9

Countless symbols signal a person's status or significance. For example, wearing a wedding ring, driving a Mercedes, or wearing shabby clothing all communicate without words. People who are most sensitive to honor and shame are keenly aware of such signs. Their meaning is rooted in history. Some cultures shame people by forcing them to wear specific hats, clothing, or placards with accusing messages. Or, if a person seeks to be king, it's common for him to wear a crown or march into a city riding a warhorse and leading his army. And yet, this is not entirely what we see in Zechariah 9 about a coming king.

Although "his dominion shall be from sea to sea, and from the River to the ends of the earth" (9:10), he is humble, bringing peace rather than destruction to the nations. In Zechariah 6:12–13, the prophet adds, "He shall build the temple of the Lord. It is he that shall build the temple of the Lord; he shall bear royal honor, and shall sit and rule on his throne." Somehow, according to Zechariah 9:9, one will ride upon a donkey, on a colt, signaling royal victory, even the restoration of David's promised kingdom.

In Matthew 21:5 and John 12:14–15, the Gospel writers claim that Jesus fulfills Zechariah 9:9 when he enters Jerusalem. The crowd not only treats him as a king; Jesus even begins to act like one when he cleanses the Temple. Throughout their accounts, the Gospels demonstrate how Christ overturns not only the Temple tables but the expectations of the people. Many ancient Jews looked for a king who would restore Israel's honor through battle and bloodshed. However, Jesus is glorified through his self-denial and death. His persistent provocations of the authorities were for peace. His triumph looks like defeat, yet his shame is turned into honor.

The Gospel writers draw from Zechariah not only to show that God is faithful to keep his promises. They also illustrate the grandeur of our human misunderstanding about what is honorable and what is lowly. In Christ, we witness the meekness of divine majesty and learn that one's worth is not determined by outward appearances but by true allegiance to God.

Parting Reflection

How do people of high status behave? What symbols signify their social position? How might Christ's followers subvert those actions and symbols to demonstrate the values of his kingdom?

Parting Prayer

Lord, we too often look for power and status in the ways of this world, whether in fame, wealth, or control. Open our eyes to see what has true significance. Change our hearts to embrace honor amid humility.

Defiling God

———————— ⑪ ————————

By offering polluted food upon my altar. But you say, "How have we polluted you?" By saying that the Lord's table may be despised.

—MAL. 1:7 ESV

Malachi 1:7 is among the most startling verses in the Bible. The text says that people pollute, defile, or desecrate God. Such vivid language itself seems almost sacrilegious. But there it is. How do we understand these words?

The people of Israel grasped what it means to show honor; they simply didn't apply this knowledge to the Lord. Although people honor fathers and respect masters, the priest despises God's name (1:6). Rather than commit overt blasphemy, the people were simply apathetic when it came to serving the Lord. It would be unimaginable to give their governors these defective gifts (1:8), yet what they offer God was inferior, leftover, or unwanted. Verse 7 summarizes their gross disregard as "polluting" God!

Contrary to contemporary thought, there is nothing private about our worship or our sin. God's people are called to be a light to the nations. Abraham's offspring are blessed to be a blessing and bear God's image in the world. A refrain echoes throughout the first chapter of Malachi: The Lord's name will be great among the nations (1:5, 11, 14). How often do we think our irreverence for the Lord affects no one but ourselves; yet, why would anyone want to honor the God whom we treat with casual indifference?

The Lord will magnify the holiness of his name, and so disciplines his people. In Malachi 2:2–3, he says:

> *If you will not listen, if you will not lay it to heart to give glory to my name, says the Lord of hosts, . . . I will rebuke your offspring, and* spread dung on your faces, *the dung of your offerings, and I will put you out of my presence* (emphasis added).

God is not concerned with external rituals. He wants internal rejoicing as we come to know him as the "great King" (1:14). What happens to those who merely go through the motions of worship? The Lord puts them to shame with excrement and exclusion (2:9)!

But there is hope for God's people, "those who revered the Lord and thought on his name. They shall be mine, says the Lord of hosts, my special possession on the day when I act, and I will spare them as parents spare their children who serve them" (3:16–17). They "shall go out leaping like calves from the stall" (4:2).

Parting Reflection

How does giving the Lord our leftovers while simultaneously giving the best of ourselves to others dishonor God? Could this charge be leveled against you? How might worshiping the Lord become casual for you?

Parting Prayer

Lord, we confess that we are prone to honor friends, celebrities, and various public figures more than we glorify you. But your Spirit changes our hearts, so we stand in awe of your name (Mal. 2:5). Through us, magnify yourself among our neighbors and the nations.

NEW

TESTAMENT

Shame in the New Testament

————————— ⑴⑾⑴ —————————

And her husband Joseph, being a just man and unwilling to put her to shame, resolved to divorce her quietly.

—MATT. 1:19 ESV

The first-century, Greco-Roman world certainly differs from that of the Old Testament. Yet, shame remains a key element to understanding the proclamation of the New Testament. Its pages contain several passages where Westerners expect to see "guilt," but the authors discuss "shame." Here are a few examples.

First, Matthew 1:19 (quoted above) involves the well-known Nativity story. While readers of Matthew's gospel are aware of the truth, Joseph did not initially know how Mary became pregnant. Understandably, he concludes that Mary had committed adultery. This would have been a direct violation of the seventh commandment and, according to Leviticus 20:10, was punishable by death. Given that legal tradition and Joseph being characterized as a "just man," we might expect the text to emphasize Mary's supposed guilt. Instead, Matthew highlights the shame associated with adultery.

Next, in 2 Thessalonians 3:14, Paul says, "Take note of those who do not obey what we say in this letter; have nothing to do with them, so that they may be ashamed." Paul admonishes the Thessalonians not to walk in idleness and provides severe directives for dealing with idlers and busybodies. Verse 14 then connects disobedience and the resulting disassociation from the community not with guilt but with shame. While they might have felt guilt, Paul chooses to highlight their feeling of shame that would, ideally, lead to repentance and restoration to the community.

Last, John writes, "And now, little children, abide in him, so that when he is revealed we may have confidence and not be put to shame before him at his coming" (1 John 2:28). In 2:27, John reminds believers that they should abide in Christ. In 2:29, he speaks of Christ's righteousness and the need for believers to practice righteousness. First John 2:28 sits between verses 27 and 29, again encouraging believers to abide in Christ. We might have expected John to say that failing to abide leaves us as transgressors of the law of Christ and thus guilty when he returns. Instead, John highlights how failing to abide in Christ leaves us feeling shame at Christ's second coming.

The New Testament authors lived in a world of shame. Thus, it is only natural that honor-shame language is pervasive throughout their writings. Being aware of this can better help us to understand both the scriptures and God himself.

Parting Reflection

The Bible speaks to both the feelings of guilt and shame. How might this fact impact your ministry? In what ways can you highlight how the gospel takes away our shame, not merely our guilt?

Parting Prayer

Father, thank you that your word speaks to the hearts of people around the world. We praise you that your gospel transcends culture. Spirit, open our eyes to see the myriad ways that sin affects us and how you both speak to those emotions.

God's Glory as the Goal of Sanctification

------------ ·⫿⫿⫿· ------------

In the same way, let your light shine before others, so that they may see your good works and give glory to your Father in heaven.

—MATT. 5:16

"Sanctification" is a common term tossed around in Christian circles. The Greek word (*hagiazō*) means "to make holy" or "to be set apart." Question 35 in the Westminster Shorter Catechism defines sanctification as "the work of God's free grace, whereby we are renewed in the whole man after the image of God, and are enabled more and more to die unto sin, and live unto righteousness." Additionally, we know from Scripture that sanctification is important to our faith (Exod. 31:13; John 17:17; 1 Thess. 4:3). So, what else does sanctification involve?

A chief concern in John 15 is that we bear fruit for God (John 15:2, 4, 5, 8, 16). Verse 8 even says that we prove to be disciples of Christ when we "bear much fruit." Jesus makes clear that to bear fruit, we must abide in him: "Those who abide in me and I in them bear much fruit, because apart from me you can do nothing" (15:5). And we abide in Christ by obeying his commandments (15:7, 10), which instruct us to love others by serving them as Christ has served us (15:12–14). As we increasingly abide in Christ in these ways, we are living out our sanctification. But is there a supreme goal to this process? Jesus suggests one in John 15:8, "My Father is glorified by this, that you bear much fruit and become my disciples."

God's glory as the goal of sanctification is not an isolated idea but can be seen throughout Scripture. Psalm 23:3 says, "He leads me in right paths *for his name's sake*" (emphasis added). While reminding believers that they are a royal priesthood that is to live holy (sanctified) lives, Peter says, "Conduct yourselves honorably among the Gentiles, so that, though they malign you as evildoers, they may see your honorable deeds and glorify God when he comes to judge" (1 Pet. 2:12). Jesus states a similar end goal for the result of our sanctified good deeds in Matthew 5:16 (quoted above): shining our light before others "so that they may see your good works and give *glory to your Father in heaven*" (emphasis added). Thus, we again see that the primary goal of our sanctification is that God would be honored.

Parting Reflection

Have you ever considered that the primary goal of your sanctification and loving others is God's glory? Do you think this end goal minimizes or enhances a genuine love for others?

Parting Prayer

We say with our Lord Jesus, "Sanctify [us] in the truth, [your] word is truth." Spirit, help us to abide in Christ and so prove to be his disciples, all to the glory of God.

Do You Want True Honor?

————————— ⑊ —————————

*And whenever you pray, do not be like the hypocrites; for they love to
stand and pray in the synagogues and at the street corners, so that
they may be seen by others. Truly I tell you, they have received their
reward. But whenever you pray, go into your room and shut the door
and pray to your Father who is in secret; and your Father who sees in
secret will reward you.*

—MATT. 6:5–6

A key existential question that could sum up these verses goes like this: "Do
you want to be holy or simply known as holy?" Or perhaps, "Do you want
to be honored or known as honored?"[46] Of course, the two are not mutually
exclusive. Still, Jesus's primary point in Matthew 6 seems to be that the Pharisees, despite the appearance of being holy and having a place of honor, are
neither truly holy nor honorable. In short, their pursuit of honor is all wrong.

Honor is gained in two ways. It can be ascribed and achieved. Ascribed
honor generally stems from factors outside one's control, such as gender or
family name. Achieved honor is gained through one's actions and accomplishments. Werner Mischke summarizes the essence of each. He says, "Ascribed
honor is more about one's being . . . On the other hand, achieved honor is more
about one's behavior."[47] Neither is inherently good or bad, better or worse.
Instead, the problem is that sin greatly distorts how we pursue honor. The
hypocrites that Jesus speaks of in the Sermon on the Mount pursued praise
from others through their pious appearances and positions. They practiced
their righteousness before others yet received no honor from God (Matt. 6:1).

———————————

46. See entry on Leviticus 10:3 for a discussion on the connection between "holiness" and
"honor."
47. Mischke, *The Global Gospel*, 94.

Although seeking honor is not inherently wrong, how we do so is important. As Christians, our ascribed honor comes not from any title or position that we were born into but from the fact that God caused us to be born again, giving us an "imperishable, undefiled, and unfading" inheritance (1 Pet. 1:3–5). Should we seek achieved honor? Yes, but our pursuit must be upside-down in comparison to the world's efforts. True honor comes only by humbling ourselves and serving others. True honor from God comes not from our outward appearances and positions, but from what is in our hearts. We must not find contentment in what others think of us. Rather, we must regularly lay ourselves bare before the Lord, receiving the honor that he bestows on us and seeking ways to humbly serve others. Then we will gain true honor.

Parting Reflection

Jesus repeats the phrase "Many who are first will be last, and the last will be first" (Matt. 19:30; 20:16). A similar idea is in Mark 10:43–44, "But whoever wishes to become great among you must be your servant, and whoever wishes to be first among you must be slave of all." What do you think Jesus means? What does it teach about the pursuit of honor in God's kingdom?

Parting Prayer

Lord, help us to seek your honor and glory first and foremost. And to whatever degree that we seek earthly greatness and honor, may we do so according to your ways.

Is the Gospel Legal or Relational?

"Who is my mother, and who are my brothers?" And pointing to his disciples, he said, "Here are my mother and my brothers! For whoever does the will of my Father in heaven is my brother and sister and mother."

—MATT. 12:48–50

How do you typically think about the gospel? How do you usually explain the gospel to others? If you grew up in a Western culture, you probably have an individualistic and legal understanding of the gospel. There is, however, another way of seeing the gospel, one that is primarily collectivistic and emphasizes group membership. Of course, these perspectives are not mutually exclusive. They complement each other beautifully. Nevertheless, we all likely have inclinations and habits of speaking. Because traditional Western Christianity tends to be individualistic, let's focus briefly on sharing the gospel with a more collectivist mindset.

Jesus offers a new identity for those who pledge their allegiance to him. When Christ saves us, he brings us into a new family. This new status is relational as it brings us to our true father and gives us innumerable brothers and sisters. Jesus emphasizes this point as a way of drawing people to his message, as in Matthew 12:48–50 (quoted above).

How do we then share the gospel with a focus on group identity? Try using more relational language instead of legal metaphors. A five-word outline for sharing the message of salvation emphasizing legal language might go like this: transgression, guilt, restitution, confession, and forgiveness. By contrast, a five-word outline for sharing the message of salvation using relational language could go like this: unfaithfulness, shame, restoration, allegiance, and honor.[48]

---

48. Georges and Baker, *Ministering in Honor-Shame Cultures*, 181.

It bears repeating that neither approach is inherently better. Both are gloriously true and present in Scripture. The gospel is both legal and relational. For example, look at Romans 3:22–25 and see if you now notice a variety of images, whether legal, honor, shame, purity and more:

> *For there is no distinction: For all have sinned and fall short of the glory of God, and are justified by his grace as a gift, through the redemption that is in Christ Jesus, whom God put forward as a propitiation by his blood, to be received by faith* (ESV).

A robust presentation of the gospel includes a spectrum of images drawn from across the Bible. Christ not only releases us from guilt; he also gives us an identity worthy of honor!

Parting Reflection

What would a 1-minute gospel presentation from a primarily honor-shame perspective sound like? Think about it for a few minutes. Perhaps even write one out.

Parting Prayer

Father, we praise you that your gospel transcends all cultures. Thank you for overcoming our shame, forgiving our transgressions, casting away our fear, and cleansing us from our impurity. You truly are a glorious God and are worthy of all honor and praise.

Filial Piety

———————— ⑇ ————————

For God said, "Honor your father and your mother," and, "Whoever
speaks evil of father or mother must surely die." But you say that who-
ever tells the father or mother, "Whatever support you might have had
from me is given to God," then that person need not honor the father.

—MATT. 15:4–5

Filial piety is a fundamental element of many Eastern cultures that can most
simply be described as respect for one's parents and elders. Many years ago,
I had the privilege of teaching a writing course to 49 students from China.
Each week, I required them to write a journal entry in a notebook. One week,
I gave a prompt that asked the students to explain the concept of filial piety
to a foreigner and describe what it means to them. Here are two samples:[49]

> "Filial piety means a kind of responsibility to me. Sometimes I should obey my
> parents' wishes, like choosing a school and major, and even choosing where I
> work . . . It requires young people to take responsibility but also makes them
> lose their independence."

> "It is an important factor in big decisions that I have made in my life. . . . If
> someday I need to choose where to work or where to live, I would choose a
> place that is near to my parents. In this way, I can take good care of them."

Filial piety concerns one's identity, viewing himself or herself as an integral part of a family group. People do not conceive of themselves as isolated
individuals with personal dreams that do not account for their community. In
many respects, this mindset is at odds with individualist cultures. As another

---

49. These quotes have been used with permission from the students who wrote them.

Chinese said, children with a concern for filial piety are "supposed to honor, respect, and take care of parent's material needs, and excel in profitable business in order for the family to gain face in other people's eyes."[50]

In Matthew 15 (quoted above), Jesus makes a case against the Pharisees for their lack of filial piety. He roots his argument in Exodus 20–21. God's word commands us to honor our parents and warns us against reviling them. While some readers today may not have an Eastern sense of filial piety instilled in them, we should still take our cue from Scripture. Filial piety was of great importance to Jesus. He demonstrated this even while hanging on the cross when he ensured that his mother would be taken care of (John 19:26–27). Similarly, we have a responsibility to honor, respect, and take good care of the needs of the parental figures in our lives. As we do this, let us view ourselves less independently and more as a part of a community.

Parting Reflection

Do you view yourself as completely independent from your father, mother, or other parental figures? What do you think it means to view yourself less as independent from your parents and more as an interdependent part of a community with them?

Parting Prayer

Father, thank you for giving us life and for always being the good Father that you are. Jesus, we praise you for being a true filial son to the Father. Spirit, help us to be true filial children of our true Father.

---

50. Carl Roberts, "Toward an Emic, Spiritually Based Perspective on Filial Piety," In *Bamboo in Mist: An Exploratory Understanding of Chinese Spirituality*, ed. Kaylene Powell (Skyforest, CA: Urban Loft, 2020), 29–31.

A Glorious Touch

─────────── ∿ ───────────

A leper came to him begging him, and kneeling he said to him, "If you choose, you can make me clean." Moved with pity, Jesus stretched out his hand and touched him, and said to him, "I do choose. Be made clean!"

—MARK 1:40–41

Leviticus 13 lists various laws for people with leprosy. One stipulation says, "The person who has the leprous disease shall wear torn clothes and let the hair of his head be disheveled; and he shall cover his upper lip and cry out, 'Unclean, unclean'" (13:45). As if this wasn't enough, lepers were also seen as ceremonially unclean and thus unfit for worship. All in all, being a leper didn't just mean physical isolation, but also spiritual and emotional isolation. Of the leprous man in Mark 1, Stephen Witmer says, "Being cut off from [the community of God's people] was like a living death. The leprous man who came to Jesus couldn't have physical contact with others, because doing so would make them unclean. Can you imagine the shame he felt?"[51]

This leper needed more than physical healing. He needed spiritual and emotional restoration. From three simple words, "and touched him," we see that Jesus must have recognized these needs. Tim Keller comments on the significance of this physical touch, saying:

> [It] must have been a response not to the physical, but to the emotional suffering of the leper. It was unnecessary for his body's healing, but the experience of leprosy was just as ravaging spiritually and emotionally . . . this man had not likely felt another human being's touch for a long time . . . [and so] we learn that Jesus does not only consider the physical side of this man's problem. He

─────────────

51. Stephen Witmer, *When Shame Keeps You Away*, https://www.desiringgod.org/articles/when-shame-keeps-you-away.

approaches the man holistically. Jesus is not above noticing and meeting a purely emotional need. Jesus gives the man more than he asked for.[52]

Frequently, the worst part of a disease or illness is the isolation that comes with it. The loss of human contact can deaden the human heart just as leprosy numbs the skin. Undoubtedly, physical healing is vital. Yet, another significant aspect of healing involves the removal of shame. In healing this man, Jesus restores a semblance of honor to him by allowing him to reenter the community of God's people. Most importantly, this powerful touch from Jesus assures the man and us that God welcomes whoever society deems unclean.

Parting Reflection

While we most likely will not physically touch someone and heal them from leprosy, how might we "touch" someone and have this same profound impact? Who in your life can you do this for now?

Parting Prayer

Lord, so often, we need more than just a physical change in circumstances. What we need is Jesus's touch. Lord, help us take whatever burden of shame we are carrying, kneel before Jesus, and ask him for his healing touch. May we also experience the honor of restoration.

---

52. Timothy J. Keller, *The Gospel of Mark: Leader's Guide*. Redeemer Presbyterian Church. 2005, https://gospelinlife.com/downloads/the-gospel-of-mark-group-study-product/.

"I Want to Be Great"

———————— ⫴ ————————

Whoever welcomes one such child in my name welcomes me, and whoever welcomes me welcomes not me but the one who sent me.

—MARK 9:37

I sought the pinnacle of status as a high school senior, and I had climbed it. I was accepted to the United States Military Academy at West Point. When asked why I chose to go there, I answered, "Because I want to be great." My ambition was matched only by my foolishness.

Little did I realize that I was playing the same competitive game as Jesus's disciples, who argued with one another about who was the greatest (Mark 9:34). Their dispute exposed a serious problem. So, Mark slows down the pace of his story. He describes how Jesus "sat down, called the twelve, and said to them, 'Whoever wants to be first must be last of all and servant of all'" (Mark 9:35). But how? We could easily overlook the significance of Jesus' answer.

In ancient Mediterranean culture, many believe that slaves held higher social status than children. One scholar explains, "people considered children fundamentally deficient and not yet human in the full sense. . . . Children occupied a low rung on the social ladder."[53] Yet, taking a child into his arms, Jesus said, "Whoever welcomes one such child in my name welcomes me, and whoever welcomes me welcomes not me but the one who sent me" (9:37). In a word, he flips the script for understanding greatness. The disciples were left baffled.

According to Jesus, greatness is about who *we* accept, *not* about who accepts us. Like the disciples, my understanding of greatness was completely backward and even self-defeating. *How can we argue about being great when*

---

53. Judith Gundry Volf, "The Least and the Greatest" in Children in the New Testament, ed. Marcia J. Bunge (Grand Rapids, MI: Eerdmans, 2001), 32.

greatness itself entails giving honor to others? When we focus on accepting outsiders rather than being accepted by so-called insiders, our ambition better honors Christ and builds unity among his people.

Parting Reflection

The longing for attention is natural, but it often becomes all-consuming until it harms both us and those around us. How have you competed for public praise at the expense of others?

Parting Prayer

Lord, you demonstrated true greatness by pouring out your life to welcome the outcast and save the lost. May our ambition be to follow your example. We confess our wayward drive to win the applause of others. We praise your name, which is above all other names.

For the Love of Honor

──────────── ⑇ ────────────

And they said to him, "Grant us to sit, one at your right hand and one at your left, in your glory."

—MARK 10:37

A love of honor involves a person's desire that others hold him or her in high esteem. Within most Eastern cultures, the opposite of shame is honor. So, it's not surprising to learn that people from those cultures have a deep-seated love for honor. Society instills this desire into children from a young age. In Chinese culture, filial piety is a social norm. A person shows respect for one's elders by seeking to be a top student and entering the best schools. Such children receive honor from their peer group. Their parents will likewise receive honor when the local community hears about their child's accomplishments.

People in Scripture also have a love of honor. With this observation, Christians can better understand sections of the Bible that are otherwise unsettling. Consider James and John's request to be seated on either side of Jesus in his kingdom. Werner Mischke comments, "This is nothing less than audacious to my Western mindset. What a blatant request for a favor from Jesus. What were James and John displaying? Love of honor!"[54] Elsewhere, this love for honor is seen when the Pharisees seek the best seat, the disciples quarrel about who is the greatest, and Jacob wrestles with God until he receives the blessing (honor!).

Western minds typically read such passages and assume that the motivations are inherently prideful and thus sinful. To be sure, pursuing honor can be sinful; however, one needs to be careful not to throw the baby out with the bathwater. An unmistakable theme in Scripture is that of God seeking his own glory. Another frequent motif is God seeking to bless creation. For

---

54. Mischke, *The Global Gospel*, 86.

example, in God's covenant with Abraham, he promises to bless Abraham and to make his name great (i.e., giving Abraham honor!).

In short, loving honor is not inherently sinful. We could say that it is just humanity's longing to return to the position of honor and glory that Adam and Eve had before the Fall.

Parting Reflection

How is the love of honor different in Eastern and Western cultures? Can you think of ways that a love for honor manifests itself in Western culture? How might it be loving?

Parting Prayer

Lord, we praise you because all honor and glory belong to you. We thank you that you will not give your glory to any other and that you defend your mighty name. Thank you for sending your Son so that we may have life and may share in your glory.

Does the Father Forsake the Son?

At three o'clock Jesus cried out with a loud voice, "Eloi, Eloi, lema sabachthani?" which means, "My God, my God, why have you forsaken me?"

—MARK 15:34

Some teachers suggest that Christ endured the ultimate shame when God the Father turned his back on the Son as he suffered unto death. They cite Jesus' words on the cross (quoted above), which is a quotation from Psalm 22:1. These impressions, however, overlook the original context of the psalm.[55] In fact, the Gospel writer's use of Psalm 22 is ironic, to say the least. This insight sheds surprising light on Jesus' message.

The psalmist, David, doesn't suggest that God utterly rejects him. Instead, he emphasizes how God is "so far from helping [him]," does *"not answer"* him, such that "[he can] find no rest" (22:1–2). David focuses on God's seeming absence, which leads to his plight. David complains of God's inaction.[56] Still, he never thinks the Lord completely rejects him (22:22–31). Not only does he expect to sing of God's deliverance, the psalmist says that God "did not despise or abhor the affliction of the afflicted, and he did not hide his face from me, but heard when I cried to him" (22:24).

Why then does Jesus quote David? In view of Psalm 22, his cry ultimately points to the hope that God will rescue him, contrary to his present pain. His shame is public but not divine. It is temporary, not permanent. In effect, Jesus signals ahead to his coming victory, like Arnold Schwarzenegger's character in *Terminator*, who says, "I'll be back."

55. Scholars well document how extensively Psalm 22 shapes Mark 15.

56. This is a common connotation of the Hebrew word translated "forsaken." See, for example, Lamentations 5:20 and Isaiah 54:7–8.

Rather than magnify Christ's utter shame, his words look forward to restored honor. The Father will resurrect the Son. As Bible scholar Richard Bauckham states, "Beyond the forsakenness, God intervened to deliver."[57] Biblical authors often use irony to shock and inspire. Mark echoes a common refrain in Scripture, depicting Christ as the righteous sufferer. Against all appearances at calvary, he will vindicate the righteous, and restore honor to all who call on him by faith.

Parting Reflection

When have you felt forsaken by God or someone else? How did you see God bring restoration and flourishing in ways you could not have expected?

Parting Prayer

Father, the pain of our suffering is real, but we confess that your faithfulness can make all things new. Just as you did not reject the Son, we rejoice that you never utterly forsake us. Grant us eyes of faith to see as Jesus saw, even while on the cross.

---

57. Richard Bauckham, *Jesus and the God of Israel* (Grand Rapids, MI: Eerdmans, 2008), Kindle loc. 3223–24.

How Jesus Labeled People

———— ⫶⫶⫶ ————

I have come to call not the righteous but sinners to repentance.

—LUKE 5:32

Labels are powerful, both for good and ill. When a doctor diagnosed me with ADHD at age 33, I found the label liberating because I finally could name and treat the specific struggle I'd had for years. However, some labels, such as "sinner," stigmatize. In Jesus' day, "sinner" referred to brazen lawbreakers. It was not a typical catch-all description of every human who ever sins. The term was used to set boundaries between insiders and outsiders. Competing groups might brand each other "sinners." Such words honor the insider and shame the outsider.

Once again, Jesus breaks convention, redefining the label. As one scholar says, "His social practice of table fellowship with sinners, a practice usually reserved for insiders, shows that in Jesus's view sinners need no longer be outsiders; he was 'un-othering the other.'"[58]

Two things stand out in how Jesus treats "sinners." First, he does not make table fellowship with others contingent on repentance. Second, although repentance is not a prerequisite for eating with Jesus, he still calls people to repent. He loves people as they are, but he also loves them so much that he doesn't want them to remain as they are. Certainly, Jesus is not afraid to call people "sinful" (Mark 8:38). However, he redefines "sinner" to designate those who reject him.

Contrast this with Paul's use of labels. In Romans 1:18–3:20, "sinner" and related ideas are applied to *everyone*. His language serves a purpose. Such

———————

58. Paul Trebilco, *Outsider Designations and Boundary Construction in the New Testament: Christian Communities and the Formation of Group Identity* (Cambridge: Cambridge University, 2017), 128. Many insights in this entry come from Trebilco's work.

universality magnifies the grandeur of God's grace for both Jews and Gentiles (Rom. 5:6–9).

Jesus and Paul strategically apply such offensive labels in different ways. At the same time, they share a common purpose. Their language becomes a compassionate invitation to their audience. For the people around Jesus, those whom society rejects as outsiders are embraced by him as insiders. For Paul's Roman readers, both Jews and Gentiles find their hope in Christ alone. Neither is in a unique position of privilege since God shows no partiality (Rom. 2:11). These two men use labels to reset group boundaries and establish new social identities. Those who were outsiders are now honored as insiders in and through Christ.

Parting Reflection

Reflect on texts such as Luke 5:29–32, 7:33–35, and 14:22–24. How do they challenge you to rethink whom you consider "insiders" and "outsiders"? How might you unwittingly treat fellow believers as outsiders?

Parting Prayer

Father, you bring people into your family from every culture and social status. We confess that we misapply labels, forgetting that we belong to Christ's kingdom. Grant us wisdom and love, Holy Spirit, so that like Christ we may "un-other the other."

Slippers and Hot Water

———————— ·⫴⫴· ————————

Do you see this woman? I entered your house; you gave me no water for my feet, but she has bathed my feet with her tears and dried them with her hair. You gave me no kiss, but from the time I came in she has not stopped kissing my feet. You did not anoint my head with oil, but she has anointed my feet with ointment.

—LUKE 7:44–46

In my first several months of living in China, I was a guest at Chinese friends' homes several times. I was often surprised when they offered me slippers and a cup of hot water as soon as I walked in the door. Initially, I wondered why either was necessary. Over time, my wife, who is Chinese, and I entertained many Chinese guests at our home. Instinctively, just before they arrived, she would tell me to make sure to have hot water ready and slippers out by the door. I fulfilled her requests dutifully, mostly just because it seemed like the culturally appropriate thing to do.

After our first year in China, we returned to America for the summer. I can remember feeling perplexed. There seemed to be a lack of hospitality when we visited friends' homes. We generally were not offered a drink or any food unless it was for a meal. I wasn't insulted or disappointed, but a strange feeling persisted, one that I couldn't quite put a finger on. I began to realize over time that the slippers and cup of hot water weren't mere cultural customs to be followed. They also served the purpose of making guests feel honored and welcomed. As I lived in China longer, offering guests slippers and some hot water when they entered our home became second nature. I no longer did it just to fulfill a cultural expectation. Instead, I truly understood the significance of these gestures. Rather than a duty, such acts of hospitality became my pleasure.

Luke 7 narrates a situation that involves hospitality, honor, love, and evidence of being truly forgiven. Simon the Pharisee invites Jesus and others to his home for a meal. However, Jesus chastises Simon for his lack of hospitality. And to everyone's surprise, he praises the actions of an unnamed sinful woman. Jayson Georges and Mark Baker offer insight: "What did she see? Simon insulted and disrespected the person she had come to honor when he did not offer Jesus customary gestures of hospitality. Shocked, and probably with a mix of anger and sadness, the woman took steps to show Jesus the honor and hospitality that Simon had not offered."[59] The point here is that hospitality in honor-shame cultures is more than simply being courteous. It is a way of showing honor to guests. While customs vary from culture to culture, the importance of such gestures does not. Peter exhorts, "Be hospitable to one another without complaining" (1 Pet. 4:9). In this way, we love people by honoring them.

Parting Reflection

What are typical ways of showing hospitality where you live? How well have you honored others by being hospitable to guests?

Parting Prayer

Lord, thank you for your word and all that it teaches us. We praise you that you choose to use us to minister to others and to be your ambassadors. Give us insight and wisdom to show hospitality well to guests in our home. Use our efforts for your glory.

---

59. Georges and Baker, *Ministering in Honor-Shame Cultures*, 99.

Honor as Love

— ⑊ —

Therefore, I tell you, her many sins have been forgiven—as her great love has shown. But whoever has been forgiven little loves little.

—LUKE 7:47 NIV

In the previous entry, we saw that hospitality is not merely a matter of being courteous. Instead, it also has to do with showing honor to guests. In Luke 7:44–46, Jesus specifies three ways that the woman in the passage honors him. In verse 47, he says that by performing these acts of honor, this woman *"loved much."* Can it be that showing honor to others equates to loving them?

In Romans 12, Paul elaborates on what a new life in the Spirit should look like. Romans 12:9–21 is filled with several brief descriptors of behaviors that should mark true followers of Christ. To no surprise, this list begins with love. Looking closer, verses 9 and 10 show us that loving others involves honoring them. "Let love be genuine" (12:9a). How? "Hate what is evil, hold fast to what is good" (12:9b). Love must not be reduced to tenderhearted affection. A fundamental aspect of love is that it is rooted in what is good and righteous and is opposed to what is evil. Paul then says, "Love one another with mutual affection" (12:10a). Again, how? "Outdo one another in showing honor" (12:10b). We don't love each other by simply expressing warm sentiments. Instead, a very practical way to show love is by intentionally honoring others.

Returning to Luke 7, the passage ends with the well-known phrase, "Whoever has been forgiven little loves little" (7:47 NIV). Certainly, this does not mean that loving others earns forgiveness. Instead, actively loving others is evidence of truly having received the forgiveness of sin. Furthermore, we can expand our understanding of the connection between honor and love by considering all of Luke 7:36–50. How did this sinful woman display her love to Jesus? She honored him by washing, kissing, and anointing his feet. In other words, she loved him by showing him honor. So, we could also rightly say, "Whoever has been forgiven little honors little."

Parting Reflection

Think of people in your life—perhaps family members, colleagues, classmates, a boss, a teacher, or your neighbors. Take a few minutes and think of some practical ways that you can show them honor. In the next day or two, apply it.

Parting Prayer

Jesus, we praise you that your love for us is not merely sentimental. Instead, you became a man, lived a perfect life, and died a horrible death on the cross to forgive our sin. Your love for us is intensely practical. Spirit, give us wisdom in knowing how we can love others by honoring them.

Positive versus Prohibitive Discipleship

He answered, "You shall love the Lord your God with all your heart, and with all your soul, and with all your strength, and with all your mind; and your neighbor as yourself."

—LUKE 10:27

The Bible can feel like a book full of restrictive rules: "Don't do this. Don't do that." Therefore, it's intriguing to see how Jesus answers the question, "Which commandment in the law is the greatest?" (Matt. 22:36): Love the Lord with all that we are.

In his summary of the law, Jesus doesn't draw a lot of restrictive boundaries. Instead, he casts a positive vision for discipleship. Disciples are called to much more than simply to avoid certain behaviors and thoughts. The Pharisees and Sadducees use prohibitive discipleship, drawing lines that determine who is good or bad, in or out. By contrast, Jesus uses positive discipleship as he continually calls people to follow him. Mark Baker writes, "If you are looking at the line and what you are allowed to do, then you are not actually looking at Jesus."[60]

These two approaches to discipleship have significantly different consequences. When laws become mere boundary lines, they beat people down with shame. The law is used as a weapon that stigmatizes. However, Jesus invites and even honors so-called "outsiders," showing them that they have a place in God's kingdom. This does not suggest that the way of Jesus is easy. As Baker notes, it's "not that we do not deal with behavior, but we don't start here. We start with Jesus."[61] Christ's demands spur his disciples to imagine a

---

60. Mark Baker, *Centered-Set Church: Discipleship and Community Without Judgmentalism* (Downers Grove, IL: IVP Academic, 2022), 209.
61. Mark Baker, 208.

world in which God reigns on earth as he does in heaven. This far richer and more encompassing vision moves us in ways that rules do not.

Jesus illustrates this by sharing the parable of the Good Samaritan (Luke 10:30–37). The priest and the Levite keep their distance from the disgraced and half-dead traveler. Yet, a socially shunned Samaritan demonstrates what it means to love one's neighbor. The story would have shamed the line-drawing Jews, whose view of God's kingdom had shrunk to fit only people like themselves. Meanwhile, it brought honor to the stigmatized Samaritans, showing that they too can belong to God.

Jesus does more than flip the common script that separated insiders and outsiders. He reorients and relativizes the search for honor. He helps us understand the law. It is an expression of God's character and spurs us to consider what living with honor means.

Parting Reflection

Do lists of rules motivate you to follow Christ? How might the desire to live with honor motivate us to love in ways that mere commands do not?

Parting Prayer

Father, we don't rejoice in rules but in the reign of Christ. We know you have put your law in our hearts (Jer. 31:33). So, help us to love you and others in ways that reflect your kingdom.

Holy Communion in Community

—————— ⫴ ——————

Do this in remembrance of me.

While back in America for a summer, I visited a church on a Sunday when they celebrated Communion. The pastor used 1 Corinthians 11 to clearly explain the purpose of the sacrament. He also warned against taking it flippantly. However, something else he said struck me. The pastor emphatically stressed that communion is primarily meant to be "between you and the Lord."

While a personal element of communion exists, it is not the complete picture. The pastor read the text through a narrower, Western lens. Living outside the West can sensitize a person to other aspects of Scripture. For me, residing in China helped to illuminate more aspects of 1 Corinthians 11. Paul heard how the Corinthians dishonored the Lord with their communion meal. His correction is both personal and communal. Personally, some were regularly taking the elements in an "unworthy manner" (1 Cor. 11:27). They did not sincerely reflect on and confess the gravity of their sin that sent the Lord Jesus to the cross, where he shed his blood and his body was broken. Western Christians rightly stress this personal aspect of honoring communion.

The second part of Paul's admonition involves the Corinthians' lack of regard for their community. Some people took too much food while others went hungry. How might we retain this concern to honor one another today? The early church shared an entire meal together. Today, many churches merely sip from a common cup or partake from a single loaf of bread. Perhaps, we could incorporate a time where members can confess their sins to one another (James 5:16). After all, communion proclaims that we live as one body, called to be broken on behalf of the world, just like our Savior.

Dietrich Bonhoeffer well captured the togetherness that should mark communion. He said:

The table of fellowship of Christians implies obligation. It is *our* daily bread that we eat, not my own. We share our bread. Thus, we are firmly bound to another not only in the Spirit but in our whole physical being. The *one* bread that is given to our fellowship links us together in a firm covenant.[62]

Parting Reflection

Have you ever considered how the cross links all Christians together? How might acknowledging this truth help us to confess sin as we prepare to take communion?

Parting Prayer

Lord, thank you for shedding your blood and breaking your body for us. The next time we take communion, O Lord, help us to properly examine ourselves. Help us to know that communion is not just between you and me. And help us to better understand that you have united all who trust in your name. Lord, may we truly take communion in a holy manner and do so together, in remembrance of you.

---

62. Dietrich Bonhoeffer, *Life Together* (New York: Harper One, 1954), 68.

Water Turned into Wine

The steward called the bridegroom and said to him, "Everyone serves the good wine first, and then the inferior wine after the guests have become drunk. But you have kept the good wine until now."

—JOHN 2:9–10

Some years ago, I was privileged to attend a very special birthday party for my father-in-law in rural China. At the center of the celebration was a feast, to which many friends and family were invited. In the weeks leading up, I watched as my in-laws agonized over the menu. They made certain to include every type of meat and food group. They even hired a prominent chef to prepare it all. Both quantity and quality were important to ensuring a successful birthday party. If they had failed to deliver this great meal, they would have felt insufferable dishonor and shame when the guests wondered why the food was either lacking in quantity or subpar in quality. Fortunately, their meticulous planning led to an abundance of delicious food, and everyone had a great time.

In John 2, we see a customary Jewish wedding banquet. However, it appears as though there was a breakdown somewhere in the planning for the wedding feast. The hosts run out of wine. Previously, I've always understood the main problem in the story this way: Guests could no longer have a good time, but then Jesus miraculously saves the day so that the party could go on. While true in some measure, that explanation is simplistic. Culturally speaking, the predicament was largely bound up in the honor of the bridegroom and bride before the guests.

The shame induced by running out of wine likely would have followed this family for the rest of their lives. Perhaps it's not hard to imagine the bridegroom being asked for the rest of his life, "Did you remember to prepare enough—?" However, with his miracle, Jesus not only provides a great quantity of wine, but also tremendous quality! In this way, Jesus brought great honor to the bridegroom and his family. For the bridegroom and his new bride, Jesus turned their story around as they went from "being the talk of the town in a shameful way to the talk of the town in a delightful way."[63]

Parting Reflection

"You have turned my mourning into dancing; you have taken off my sackcloth and clothed me with joy" (Ps. 30:11). Have you had experiences in life where the Lord reversed something that should have been shameful and instead poured blessing and honor on you? In what ways has he turned your mourning into dancing?

Parting Prayer

God, we thank you that you are the one who both sees and meets all our needs. As we marvel at the miracle of turning water into wine, make us see more clearly the interpersonal and social aspects of this miracle, which demonstrates your robust love and care for us.

---

63. Matthew Williams, "*Shame Removed; Honor Received, Part 1*," https://www.biola.edu /blogs/good-book-blog/2011/shame-removed-honor-received-part-1.

Unlock the Door

———— ·‖‖‖· ————

God did not send the Son into the world to condemn the world, but so that the world might be saved through him... those who do not believe are condemned already, because they have not believed in the name of the only Son of God.

—JOHN 3:17–18

By the time Jack realized he was having a severe allergic reaction, his skin was bright red, and his face looked like a bulldog. Speaking with the 911 operator, his voice cracked as his throat began swelling, each word slowly suffocating him. Help was on the way, but the operator told Jack he must do one thing before they arrived: *Go unlock the door.* If he wanted to receive the rescue, he had to unlock the door. The operator didn't try to convince Jack that he didn't have an allergy or that he wasn't dying on the phone as they spoke. She also didn't scold him but rather told him the responsible step he must take to be saved.

By contrast, some people are so desperate to eliminate shame that they deny the doors that need to be unlocked. Many unhelpful strategies exist to deal with shame. A popular one is to free people of responsibility by blaming genetics or one's environment. Sometimes, that's right, but not always. Christians often quote John 3:16 ("For God so loved the world . . ."), explaining that God loves us just as we are. But this famous verse only tells part of the story of healing.

We can't eliminate shame by pinning blame elsewhere, whether on parents, corporations, or systems. That's precisely how shame works—blame-shifting—and it's always counterproductive. This response perpetuates the lie that our worth depends on minimizing our flaws and failures. Instead, we combat shame by recognizing that weak, flawed, and sinful people still have worth. This applies to dieters, drunks, and delinquents. The cure is not to render people as powerless victims to nature and nurturing.

We must keep reading to John 3:17–18 (quoted above). Jesus acknowledges that some stand condemned already and that everyone in the world needs saving. Despite this, verse 16 is true. God does love the whole world, and he did send his Son to set us free from sin and shame. But we still must place our faith in him, putting our lives in his hands. We must go unlock the door to receive his rescue.

Parting Reflection

Have you ever utilized blame-shifting to explain away characteristics about your life that you're ashamed of? Why is it sometimes hard to accept that weak, flawed, and sinful people still have worth? How does John 3:16–18 help?

Parting Prayer

Father, we are in awe of your love. We have worth simply because you love us. Christ bought us with his blood. Help us to see that while you love us, ashamed sinners, you also love us too much to leave us that way.

Does Jesus Shame
the Samaritan Woman?

———————— ᯤ ————————

Jesus said to her, "You are right in saying, 'I have no husband'; for you have had five husbands, and the one you have now is not your husband. What you have said is true!"

—JOHN 4:17–18

The Samaritan woman in John 4 has a bad reputation, but it has not always been that way. Biblical scholar Lynn Cohick says, "For most early church and medieval interpreters, the Samaritan woman was a careful, polite seeker—a sinner who, once illumined, truthfully witnessed her new faith to others. But in the Reformation, she became a symbol of promiscuity."[64] Have modern readers sullied the Samaritan woman's reputation? How does John present her?

Many people use John 4:17–18 (quoted above) to support their assumption that the woman is a serial adulteress. However, Cohick and others show this assumption to be baseless. Several historical factors could have contributed to this admittedly unusual situation. A few husbands might have died prematurely. Perhaps one or two men divorced her. Maybe her circumstances forced her into the role of a concubine. One can't be sure, but we are confident a serial adulteress would never find so many men willing to marry her if she had such a stained reputation.

In addition, John depicts the woman in surprisingly positive terms, despite being a Samaritan, an apostate outcast in the eyes of typical Jews. To start, she demonstrates more theological curiosity than perhaps anyone else in John's

---

64. Lynn Cohick, "Was the Samaritan Woman Really an Adulteress?" *Christianity Today.* October 2015.

Gospel. Next, she engages with Jesus despite the social stigma attached to a woman's speaking with a Jewish teacher (4:27). Finally, she is so eager to share news of Jesus that she leaves behind her water jar as she hastily returns to the city.

Even more staggering, "Many Samaritans from that city believed in him because of the woman's testimony" (4:39). In the ancient Mediterranean world, many men questioned the reliability of women's testimony. Yet, the townspeople somehow respected her enough not only to follow up on her claims but to believe in Jesus as Savior of the world! This is hardly what we'd expect if the Samaritan woman were a shameless social pariah.

Another clue suggests that John wants us to esteem the Samaritan woman. Literarily, John juxtaposes Jesus's daytime conversation with the woman with his nighttime interaction with Nicodemus. John often uses light and darkness to convey positive and negative connotations, respectively.

Parting Reflection

Jesus does not shame the Samaritan woman. Instead, he breaks with social convention to show her honor and brings the gospel to stigmatized people. What assumptions about other people lead us to disrespect or dishonor them? How might we perpetuate prejudice or sexism?

Parting Prayer

Jesus, how might you surprise us, even today, if we would be slow to assume the worst in others? Open our hearts to show people grace and listen to their stories. You are Savior of the world!

Do You Really Believe?

———————— ⑈ ————————

So his brothers said to him, "Leave here and go to Judea so that your disciples also may see the works you are doing; for no one who wants to be widely known acts in secret. If you do these things, show yourself to the world." (For not even his brothers believed in him.)

—JOHN 7:3–5

To borrow from Thoreau, the masses of people lead lives of quiet desperation to be known. When they don't get the public acclaim they want, people "borrow face." This Chinese expression means that we will ride the coattails of people with a better reputation or social status than us. Businesses use celebrity endorsements, while ordinary people like to name-drop. Is it possible that we do something like this with Jesus?

In John 7, Jesus's brothers urge him to do great works that will bring him more glory and followers. Their counsel sounds more than reasonable; it seems wise. Doesn't God want the world to honor Jesus? However, John surprises us by saying, "not even his brothers believed in him." John hints that Jesus's brothers have an ulterior motive. They seek their own glory *through* him. The brothers want to use him to boost their own social status. Their real goal is not glory for Jesus but for themselves. Their advice misunderstands the nature of public attention. Not all glory is created equal. According to Jesus, their misguided ambition exposes a lack of faith. Elsewhere he asks, "How can you believe when you accept glory from one another and do not seek the glory that comes from the one who alone is God?" (5:44).

Let's pause and ask, what does Jesus mean by this? John 7:18 sheds light on the difference between genuine and false faith. Jesus's opponents attempt to disparage his reputation as a teacher. Jesus responds, "Those who speak on their own seek their own glory; but the one who seeks the glory of him who sent him is true, and there is no unrighteousness in him."[65] Why does he say this? Leaders had criticized Jesus for healing a man on the Sabbath. Ironically, doing God's will detracts from Jesus's standing in the eyes of the authorities. If Jesus merely sought public praise, he would not have done this miracle. These social influencers confuse their status with God's. Such confusion inevitably leads to hypocrisy when our ambitions conflict with God's will.

Like Jesus's brothers, we can confuse chasing honor with seeking God's will. For example, we may want to attract more people to our church, so we either promote or demur certain social issues that may not be in line with God's will. We conflate his glory with ours. We confuse public attention and the number of followers with faithfulness. In what ways may we be like Jesus's brothers? Where do we lack faith, using ministry or Christian behaviors to bolster our own reputation rather than God's renown?

Parting Reflection

Faith is essential for following Christ and giving honor to God. We express our trust and allegiance in various ways. We rejoice in the things we believe in. How have you seen others rejoice in ways that made clear that their faith is in Christ?

Parting Prayer

Apart from you, Jesus, all boasting or rejoicing is in vain. Knowing you is what ultimately matters. Spirit, help us to see the glory of Christ with greater clarity and joy. May you be honored as we grow in this faith.

---

65. Adapted from NRSV.

When Outsiders Become Insiders

—————— ·∥∥∥· ——————

All that the Father gives me will come to me, and whoever comes to me I will never cast out.

—JOHN 6:37 ESV

In the ancient world, few people suffered more than those with disabilities. The stigma could lead to being ostracized from society. In John 9, people assumed the man's blindness is the consequence of someone's sin. After he was healed, the Pharisees interrogate him about Jesus, who had restored the man's sight. Unsatisfied with his answer, these leaders question the healed man's parents. Yet even they seem to distance themselves from their son because they fear being *put out of* the synagogue.

Nevertheless, the man tells the Pharisees about Jesus. "They answered him, 'You were born in utter sin, and would you teach us?' And they cast him out" (9:34). Although healed, he sees no one who will stand by his side. Jesus then reorients the Pharisees' understanding of disability. It is they, who deny their need, who are truly blind (9:41).

By contrast, Jesus seeks and finds the man, still overlooked by society. In John 10, Jesus helps us to interpret the events of John 9, explaining that he overturns social expectations.[66] He compares himself to a shepherd saying, "The sheep hear his voice, and he calls his sheep by name and leads them out. When he has brought out all his own, he goes before them, and the sheep follow him, for they know his voice" (10:3–4). The same root word translated "brought out" appears in 9:34–35 and highlights a recurring theme throughout John (6:37; 9:22; 12:42–43; 16:2).

---

66. Readers might overlook this point if they forget that the chapter divisions were added many centuries after John wrote his Gospel.

What is Jesus saying? The sheep who are outside the pen with the Shepherd are "insiders" in Jesus's eyes. Those who are considered "outsiders" by society are welcomed as insiders in God's family! Now, *outsiders have a place of honor*! We need not fear being cast aside by others or ignored by so-called people of influence. Jesus reverses conventional notions of status. He can set aside whatever causes anxiety and despair. Although the world can be confusing, scary, and hurtful, we are called simply to follow the good Shepherd's voice.

Parting Reflection

How have you felt and responded in times when you felt like an outsider? For cultural reasons, we might unwittingly treat fellow brothers and sisters in Christ as though they are outsiders. Have you witnessed others being treated as social outsiders? Have you seen this in the church? How might you overturn typical notions of honor and shame in your community so that you welcome cultural "outsiders" as kingdom insiders?

Parting Prayer

We confess that, at times, we've subtlety excluded or disregarded people for countless reasons. But we embrace your forgiveness, Father, and rejoice that you welcome us into your family because of Christ. Grant us boldness to follow the Shepherd's voice wherever he leads.

Judas Had a Seat of Honor

———————— ·||||· ————————

So while reclining next to Jesus, he asked him, "Lord, who is it?" Jesus answered, "It is the one to whom I give this piece of bread when I have dipped it in the dish." So when he had dipped the piece of bread, he gave it to Judas son of Simon Iscariot.

—JOHN 13:25–26

When people think of Jesus's final meal with his disciples, many conjure an image of Leonardo da Vinci's famous portrait *of The Last Supper*. History, however, paints a different picture. People reclined on their left elbow at ancient banquets, leaving their right hand free to handle and pass food to those on either side of them. Participants also angled their bodies with their feet away from the table. Thus, one could lay his head on the chest of the guest lying to his left.

As with most cultures, ancient Mediterranean society ascribed honor to specific seats at the table. For example, one might vie to sit at the host's right or left. These were typically seen as places of honor and often assigned by the host (cf. Mark 10:37, 40). At the Lord's last supper, the disciple John seems to lie at Jesus's right (John 13:23, 25). But who is on Jesus's left? According to John 13:26, it appears to be Judas, the man who will betray him. And Jesus even *knows* Judas will betray him (John 6:64; 13:11). Still, he gives Judas a seat of honor. Not only this, but Jesus also gives Judas the special responsibility of tending the moneybag (13:29).

Although Jesus bestows extraordinary honor on him, Judas is shameless. He projects an image in public as a devotee of Jesus, working alongside other disciples to feed the hungry. Meanwhile, he steals from the funds meant for the poor (12:6). Judas is enamored with both cash and the crowd. He sells Jesus for 30 coins and a few minutes of attention from the social elites.

Simply holding a place of privilege or honor, and demonstrating high social status, does not suggest anything about someone's character. Their outward position does not indicate they have it all together. Two men sat in seats of honor to Jesus's right and left. One followed Jesus into exile. The other condemned him with a kiss to face execution on a Roman cross. How shameful for both teacher and student when a disciple betrays his master! Yet, even knowing Judas's duplicity, Jesus gave Judas a seat of honor.

Judas acted so shamelessly despite being given a place of honor. We are amazed that Jesus gave Judas an honored position despite his deceitfulness. These observations raise questions for us. How do we respond knowing that Jesus honors us by grace? John grew in humility; Judas gained hubris and was finally put to shame (Matt. 27:3–5). And how do we treat those who betray us? Do we show them respect as people loved by God, hoping that such kindness will lead them to repentance (Rom. 2:4)?

Parting Reflection

Grace is never deserved. We have enjoyed honor in times when we have acted shamefully. How have you shown similar grace to others in your life?

Parting Prayer

Jesus, your kindness amazes us. Lord, your mercies are new every day, and yet we take so much for granted. We use your name and your gifts in ways that suit us but do not necessarily exalt you. Thank you for your infinite compassion. Spirit, make us walk more like Christ.

Jesus Lovingly Shames Peter

———————— ⑁ ————————

Jesus said to him the third time, "Simon son of John, do you love me?"
Peter felt hurt because he said to him the third time, "Do you love me?"
And he said to him, "Lord, you know everything; you know that I love
you." Jesus said to him, "Feed my sheep."

—JOHN 21:17

"What were you thinking? You're so stupid." "You always mess things up."
These are just a few of the messages I and others grew up hearing as children.
They filled us with toxic shame, enough to require much of our adulthood to
clean up. Whatever our moral failings, Peter certainly can empathize with the
residual pain that follows regret and the fear of rejection. He had previously
boasted that he loved Jesus more than the other disciples did, yet he denies
the Lord three times at Jesus's most dire moment. Peter is then overcome
with sorrow when the rooster crows. He knows that he messed up. And now,
in John 21, he stands face to face with Jesus, who asks Peter three times, "Do
you love me?"

Jesus meets Peter with grace.[67] He demonstrates a healthy use of shame.
Jesus doesn't focus on what Peter did and why he did it. He doesn't call him
stupid or ask what he was thinking. Instead, Jesus concentrates on who Peter
loves. Rather than emphasize Peter's failures and flaws, Jesus emphasizes
their connection, Peter's love for Jesus, and thus his calling moving forward.
He doesn't define Peter by his mistakes, but Jesus also doesn't pretend that
Peter has his life altogether.

Jesus's use of shame is constructive, appealing to Peter's sense of identity.
The Lord does not fixate only on the past, including all that Jesus died to

---

67. This entry was inspired by and draws from Warren Williams's sermon at Redemption
Church Tempe in Tempe, Arizona on April 3, 2022.

forgive; instead, Jesus reminds Peter of all that he is saved for. Three times, Peter is told to take care of Jesus's sheep, his people. The Lord doesn't save people and put us on his team only to let us watch from the bench. No, he has a purpose for us. This is far more than a passive interest in our avoiding harm and hardship.

What's more, Jesus prepares Peter to overcome future situations that will tempt him again to forsake Christ. Although Peter will experience social shame as a follower of Christ, he need not feel personal shame. He belongs to Jesus. He is given a mission. And likewise, with us—Jesus meets our shame with grace. We belong to him. Even now, we are called to join his mission.

Parting Reflection

What is something you are ashamed of? Pause to imagine yourself in Peter's place. How do Jesus's words challenge the condemning and shaming messages in your head and your past?

Parting Prayer

Lord Jesus, you know we love you. You invite us to draw near and join you in showing steadfast love to the world. Use us as instruments of reconciliation, overcoming the shame that isolates and enslaves.

In the Name of Jesus

──────────── ·◦||||◦· ────────────

There is salvation in no one else, for there is no other name under heaven given among mortals by which we must be saved.

—ACTS 4:12

In *Harry Potter*, people are afraid even to say the name "Voldemort." Some cultures believe that speaking certain names invokes power, like a magical force. Among contemporary Christians, "the name of Jesus" often is little more than a formula tagged to the end of a prayer. For Luke, however, few words are as significant as "name," particularly when referring to Jesus.[68] In Acts 2:38, he recounts Peter's message, "Repent, and be baptized every one of you in the name of Jesus Christ so that your sins may be forgiven; and you will receive the gift of the Holy Spirit."

In many Western cultures, a person's name has little significance. However, in ancient cultures, a person's name represents their reputation, being, and identity. The Lord defines the church's mission in terms of his name. In Acts 9:13–14, Ananias expresses concern about approaching Saul, who persecutes the church and "has authority from the chief priests to bind all who *invoke your name*" (emphasis added). In reply, "the Lord said to him, 'Go, for he is an instrument whom I have chosen to bring my name before Gentiles and kings and before the people of Israel; I myself will show him how much he must suffer *for the sake of my name*'" (9:15–16 emphasis added). To bring the Lord's name to the nations entails far more than passing along information akin to sharing a social media post. Instead, Paul announces God's kingdom even among society's most influential figures (Acts 28:31). No wonder he

─────────────

68. He uses the Greek word for "name" (ὄνομα) ninety-four times. In the New Testament, over forty percent of the word's occurrences appear in Luke's Gospel or Acts.

suffered. It's no surprise that the disciples are repeatedly warned not to speak in Jesus's name (Acts 4:17–18; 5:28, 40).

What does God seek to achieve? In Acts 15:13–14, James says, "My brothers, listen to me. Simeon has related how God first looked favorably on the Gentiles, to take from among them *a people for his name*" (emphasis added). As we saw in Exodus 20:7, bearing the Lord's name signifies ownership and belonging. He wants people from all nations to join his kingdom family. The Lord wants his people to reflect his honor in all the world. This mission explains why Paul and Barnabas "risked their lives *for the name of our Lord Jesus Christ*" (Acts 15:26 ESV emphasis added).

Parting Reflection

We often go about our days as though nothing were at stake but our own well-being. It's easy to forget that we don't merely represent ourselves. How often do you give more thought to making yourself known rather than spreading Christ's glorious name? How can you "put on Christ" and "carry his name" today?

Parting Prayer

Lord Jesus, we thank you for making us *your people.* We confess that we are not our own. Spirit, grant us wisdom and boldness to endure hardship for the sake of Christ's name.

Rejoicing in Dishonor

─────────── ⫴⫴ ───────────

Then they left the presence of the council, rejoicing that they were counted worthy to suffer dishonor for the name.

—ACTS 5:41

When Jesus was arrested, his closest friends scattered. One was literally scared naked (Mark 14:51–52). These disciples had debated about who among them was the greatest. Peter had boasted that he would never desert Jesus, even if everyone else did. Yet, soon after that, he denied Jesus three times. Fast-forward just weeks later, and we see a stunning transformation. The authorities repeatedly warn the disciples not to speak in Jesus's name. Although imprisoned and threatened, the disciples persist, which enrages the council. Why do the apostles have this boldness, and what provokes such anger in response?

First, Peter challenges the honor of the high priest and the elders of Israel, saying, "We must obey God rather than any human authority." Such a daring challenge to their position was scandalously offensive. Who were these followers of Jesus, who presume to know God's will better than the temple elites? The apostles further assail the honor of Israel's leaders, saying, "The God of our ancestors raised up Jesus, whom you had killed by hanging him on a tree" (5:30). This claim asserts that the council departed from God and the ways of their ancestors, an inflammatory accusation for sure. They murdered the one whom "God exalted . . . at his right hand as Leader and Savior that he might give repentance to Israel and forgiveness of sins" (5:31).

The council then wants to kill the apostles, yet a Pharisee "named Gamaliel, a teacher of the law held in honor by all the people" persuades them otherwise. It is Gamaliel's exalted social status that compels these influential leaders to take his words seriously. So, instead of executing them, the council flogs the disciples and "ordered them not to speak in the name of Jesus" (5:40).

Honor and shame weave throughout Acts 5, but it's verse 41 that shocks our sensibilities. How do people rejoice at being considered worthy of suffering dishonor for the name of Jesus? In short, Christ's followers seek honor by representing him in the world, whether in their speech, service, or suffering.

This alternative standard of honor relativizes every other court of public opinion. Being mistreated like Jesus, because of Jesus, and for Jesus signals their genuine devotion to the King of kings. Enduring unjust persecution is their way of publicly exclaiming the worth of Christ. Were it their ambition to be esteemed by the social authorities, they would have set aside the joy that comes with true honor. Instead, as Peter later says, "If you are insulted for the name of Christ, you are blessed, because the Spirit of glory and of God rests upon you" (1 Pet. 4:14).

Parting Reflection

Do you rejoice when you're excluded and criticized for following Christ? Or do you become angry and complain about your rights? How might you suffer social shame not because you represent Christ but instead use his name to justify your agenda and reputation?

Parting Prayer

Holy God, you are worthy of unique honor. Embolden us to magnify your name by forsaking the disgraceful allurements that often come with public praise and acceptance. Change our perspective about what is worthy of praise or shame.

Honor by Suicide?

———— ·|||||· ————

When the jailer woke up and saw the prison doors wide open, he drew
his sword and was about to kill himself, since he supposed that the
prisoners had escaped . . ."Sirs, what must I do to be saved?"

—ACTS 16:27, 30

Why does the Philippian jailer intend to kill himself? Some say that he feared
the impending punishment from the merciless Roman leaders for allowing the
prisoners to escape. While plausible, that might not be the primary reason.
An aspect of Japanese culture could shed light on the situation.

In June 1945, the Japanese soldiers fighting in the Battle of Okinawa knew
that defeat was certain. For Lieutenant General Isamu Cho, this was too much
to bear. Moments before taking his own life, he dictated his own epitaph,
"Twenty-second day, sixth month, 20th year of Showa era. I depart without
regret, fear, shame, or obligation. Age on departure 51 years."[69] What moti-
vated this disposition?

Seppuku is a Japanese term for when a person voluntarily commits suicide
to maintain or restore honor as the result of a defeat in battle or to "assume
moral and legal responsibility for one's mistakes, blunders and wrong doings
as well as misconducts of one's subordinates."[70] A key driver in such decisions
is the impending change in social status as a result of one's blunder. Japanese
scholar Toyomasa Fuse describes *seppuku* as "altruistic suicide," noting that
"shame and chagrin are so extreme among the Japanese, especially in a perceived threat to loss of social status, that the individual cannot contemplate life

---

69. Lily Rothman, "The Gory Way Japanese Generals Ended Their Battle on Okinawa," *TIME*
Magazine (June 22, 2015), https://time.com/3918248/okinawa-ended-1945-history/.
70. Toyomasa Fuse, "Suicide and Culture in Japan: A Study of Seppuku as an Institutionalized
Form of Suicide." *Social Psychiatry* 15 (1980): 60.

henceforth, and rather than face the necessity of continuing life in an altered or degraded social role, he chooses to end it all."[71] In many respects, this is viewed as gaining honor by suicide. This no doubt describes Lieutenant General Cho's motivation, and perhaps the Philippian jailer's motivation as well.[72]

The threat of social shame can be debilitating; however, it is often misplaced. The Philippian jailer initially viewed his social shame from a wholly horizontal, earthly perspective. While we don't know exactly what was said, Paul and Silas must have conveyed to him that the only honor that truly matters is that which comes from God and that the Father sent his Son to die for our shame so that we may be raised to glory for eternity. Joining God's family also gave the Philippian jailer a new community, one in which everyone has honor from God. He initially feared the shame and diminished social status from his workplace blunder, but later traded honor by suicide for true, eternal honor from the King.

Parting Reflection

Do you ever look to your social status as means of defining your self-worth? If you lost your current social status, how do you think you'd be impacted?

Parting Prayer

Lord, we confess that we often over-value the opinions of others and under-value the reality of what you have accomplished for us. Help us rejoice and find contentment in the glory that is ours through Christ and as a part of your family.

---

71. Fuse, 62.

72. For a fuller explanation of the Philippian jailer's motivation, see Georges and Baker, *Ministering in Honor-Shame Cultures*, 184–186.

Intolerance with Shaming

———— ·⫴⫴· ————

When Paul came to the steps, the violence of the mob was so great that he had to be carried by the soldiers. The crowd that followed kept shouting, "Away with him!"

—ACTS 21:35–36

The internet is a petri dish for festering shame. By 2020, "canceling" became a common phrase referring to a mass effort to condemn someone's words or actions, often resulting in the person losing their job or status. Such online shaming seemingly attempts to erase social "offenders" from existence. Ironically, many people are canceled because *they* are deemed "intolerant" when, in fact, they might just disagree with popular views.

Today's context vastly differs from Paul's, but his trial story highlights how one might respond to broad efforts to shame and silence Christ's followers. Paul's faith in Christ turns him into a nonconformist traitor in the eyes of the Jewish authorities. For that, they try to kill him. Gross and unjust accusations fuel public outrage (Acts 21:21, 28–29). Feeling threatened, the leaders couldn't tolerate a challenge to social norms and traditions.

Rather than rant about how they misunderstand him, Paul humbly goes out of his way to appease concerns and clarify his intentions (21:22–26). Throughout his trial, he tries to be more patient than provocative. Both when teaching and during his interrogation, Paul is winsome and respectful, however callous or corrupt his audience. Because his character is beyond reproach, Paul doesn't fear public scrutiny, speaking openly about his life and convictions. He only invokes his rights when whipping and death loom near (22:25; 25:11). He doesn't slander or shame the political powers for his undeserved beating and arrest.

Like those who persecuted Paul, many people today feel threatened by disagreement. Their intolerance triggers a perpetuating cycle of shame attacks. Some Christians are tempted to retaliate in like manner. Yet, the lives of Jesus and Paul temper such harmful inclinations. We are called to be tolerant of people but intolerant of the shaming tactics that mark the world. Lesslie Newbigin reminds us, "We must begin by distinguishing toleration from neutrality or indifference."[73] We are not neutral, for Christ is king. While indifference fails to convey that we value others, genuine tolerance honors people as valued in God's eyes, even when they, like us, fall short. Paul demonstrates how to respond to public shaming, not with more shame but with honor.

Parting Reflection

What situations or topics can make you feel defensive and more inclined to respond with shaming? How can you show honor to those with whom you most disagree?

Parting Prayer

Christ Jesus, we have failed to be generous and humble when others disagree or challenge us. Spirit, we need the wisdom to discern the way of Christ. Grant us the courage to endure unkind words and unjust treatment for your name's sake.

---

73. Lesslie Newbigin, *Foolishness to the Greeks: The Gospel and Western Culture* (Grand Rapids, MI: Eerdmans, 186), 173.

Honoring with Honor

So when this was done, others also, which had diseases in the island, came, and were healed. Who also honored us with many honors; and when we departed, they laded us with such things as were necessary.

—ACTS 28:9–10 KJV

After nearly five years of working at a university in China, I had built a strong working relationship with a Chinese professor. I helped her out on many occasions, and we even co-taught courses over the years. When our time to leave drew near, she invited my family over to her home for a Friday night dinner. Unbeknownst to me, she had taken the entire day off work and invited about ten of her graduate students to her home to prepare an overly abundant and lavish spread for dinner. Why did she do this? Sure, she wanted to show honor to me, and that she did. Beyond that though, it was her way of expressing her thankfulness. After we left that city, she never wrote me a card nor do I recall her directly saying, "Thank you," for anything. Yet, I will always remember that dinner as her "Thank you."

In Acts 28, Paul was shipwrecked along with others who found themselves on the island of Malta. The native people were very kind, but when a viper bit Paul they thought he must be some sort of a criminal. Yet, Paul was fine, and so they decided he was a god! Paul was then brought to the father of the chief man of the island, Publius, because his father was very ill. Paul healed Publius's father along with the rest of the island's people who had various diseases (Acts 28:1–9).

In many versions of the Bible, Acts 28:10 says something like, "They also honored us greatly." The King James Version, quoted above, offers a different translation. Your Bible may have a footnote that offers an alternate translation similar to the KJV—"honored us with many honors." In fact, the Greek word translated as "honor" is used back-to-back in this clause. What can we infer from this?

No doubt the people from Malta were grateful to Paul and his companions for God's mighty work shown among them. They wanted to express their thankfulness and did so by putting whatever supplies they needed aboard the ship (28:10). This act was similar to what my Chinese colleague did for me with the lavish dinner party. The people from Malta showed their gratitude to Paul and his company by providing exceedingly for them, thus honoring them with many honors.

Parting Reflection

Have you ever considered that showing "excessive" honor to someone may be another way to express gratefulness? Think of someone to whom you want to express gratitude. What might it look like to "honor them with many honors?"

Parting Prayer

Lord, we praise you for lavishing the riches of your grace upon us (Eph. 1:8). Spirit, make us sensitive to this reality, and may we show our gratefulness by honoring you with many honors.

Sin as Dishonor

———————— ⃰|||||⃰ ————————

You who boast in the law dishonor God by breaking the law. For, as it is written, "The name of God is blasphemed among the Gentiles because of you."

—ROM. 2:23–24

"Sin" is a vague word for many people. In the West, it's often described as "missing the mark." Perhaps you've heard before that "sin" is an archery term, reserved for when arrows miss their target. It doesn't matter how much or how little it is off-target. Any miss is a "sin." In other words, "missing the mark" is rather black and white, and this often leads to a predominantly legal understanding of sin. In China, by contrast, people have a hard time understanding "sin," because the word for sin (*zuì*) means "crime." This translation confuses someone who doesn't come from a Christianized culture. Calling people "criminals" often evokes a dismissive response to the gospel.

However, notice how Paul speaks of sin. He uses honor and shame to explain both the root and fruit of sin. In Romans 1:21–25, Paul describes unrighteousness as not honoring God or giving thanks to him. Such people exchange the glory of the immortal God for images of created things. Consequently, God gives them up to the dishonoring of their bodies. It is noteworthy that in Romans 1:18–32, Paul describes unrighteousness using honor-shame, not legal, language.

Romans 2:23–24 (quoted above) is remarkable. The main verb in the sentence is "dishonor." The phrase "by breaking the law" is a preposition, not a verb. In other words, the root of sin is dishonoring God. Breaking the law is merely one specific way that Paul's Jewish opponents dishonor God. Thus, breaking the law is a fruit, not the root, of sin. Verse 24 underscores the point that honor and shame are central concerns for Paul. After all, God's honor among the nations is at stake!

Romans 3:23 might be the most famous verse in the Bible on sin. Paul says all have sinned and lack *the glory of God*. Sin fundamentally concerns a lack of glory. Sin does not glorify God because it doesn't express trust in him (Rom. 4:20; 14:23). Again, sin is far more than law-breaking.

Christ's followers desire more than law-keeping. The goal of obedience is to honor God. Consider Paul's robust vision for the Christian life. He says, "So, whether you eat or drink, or whatever you do, do everything for the glory of God" (1 Cor. 10:31). Paul doesn't want us to settle for mere innocence, as if not "missing the mark" in a legal sense were the same as worshipping God with all of life. Instead, all of life is all for Jesus, and whatever does not reflect that truth is sin. Thus, the heart of sin is dishonoring God, and we miss that mark in myriad ways.

Parting Reflection

How have you typically understood sin? How does it differ from the above discussion? How might you use everyday language to explain it to someone else?

Parting Prayer

We confess that we do not honor you with everything. Spirit, open our eyes to see sin as you see it. Then may we rejoice even more in the One who bore our sin. Indeed, all of life is all for you. We declare that you, Jesus, are the king of the world, nations, businesses, neighborhoods, and even our bathrooms.

Subjected to Shame
in the Hope of Glory

———————— ·⑴⑴⑴· ————————

For the creation was subjected to futility, not of its own will but by the will of the one who subjected it, in hope that the creation itself will be set free from its bondage to decay and will obtain the freedom of the glory of the children of God.

—ROM. 8:20–21

Have you ever asked, "Why did God make me like this?" Most of us have physical traits or other abnormalities that we wish we could change. Perhaps it's a health condition, a physical disability, barrenness, or just the way we look in general. These deficiencies can leave us feeling self-conscious and ashamed before others. Yet, God is completely sovereign over all details of creation, even those that may be unsightly or despised by society. Both human sin and Satan (Luke 13:11) can indeed bring about these "shameful" conditions. However, most of the time, these ailments are just simply the way God created us. But why? Romans 8 can help.

In verses 1–17, Paul celebrates the gift of the Spirit to believers and proclaims that we are "joint heirs with Christ—if, in fact, we suffer with him so that we may also be glorified with him" (8:17). He then extends the suffering to the creation itself in 8:18–25 (partially quoted above). While nature itself is certainly on Paul's mind, the way God has created each of us is present as well. In other words, we too have been "subjected to futility" during our time on earth (8:20). Again, why?

We have been subjected to futility in this temporary life in hope that we would be set free, knowing that we will one day be honored as Christ brings us into his glory (8:20–21). Therefore, we look to Christ in our socially shamed conditions, knowing that he is more valuable than any treasure we could have in this life and that he will one day transform our "slight momentary affliction" into an "eternal weight of glory" (2 Cor. 4:17).[74]

While we may question why God made us a certain way, we must never dwell there. Our identity must not be in our appearance or any condition in which we find ourselves. Instead, we look to Christ, knowing that he will reverse our current status. After all, there was nothing honorable about Jesus's physical appearance (Isa. 53:2). In a very real sense, he understands our condition. He went to the cross to bear our sin and shame to give us new life and hope. His death and resurrection have ended our temporary subjection to shame and created for us the hope of glory.

Parting Reflection

Have you ever wanted to change something about the way God created you? How can looking to the hope that we have in Christ impact our disposition toward whatever socially "shamed" condition we find ourselves in?

Parting Prayer

Father, we confess that we often wallow in the mire of our temporary conditions, ignoring the realities of the glory that awaits us. Jesus, we praise you for bearing our sin and shame on the cross, through which you have reconciled us to yourself. Spirit, continue to bear witness with our spirit that we are children of God.

---

74. For further reflection, consider Romans 8:24–25; 2 Corinthians 4:7–12; 1 Peter 1:13.

Whose Are We?

———————— ⑊ ————————

What I mean is that each of you says, "I belong to Paul," or "I belong to Apollos," or "I belong to Cephas," or "I belong to Christ." Has Christ been divided? Was Paul crucified for you? Or were you baptized in the name of Paul?

—1 COR. 1:12–13

The Ohio State-Michigan football matchup is colloquially known simply as "The Game." Fans from neighboring states make no secret about where their allegiances lie. On Ohio State's campus during game week, the letter "M" is crossed out on every single sign. On Michigan's campus, fans walk through a local cemetery and visit the graves of famous Wolverines. While some traditions are harmless fun, overzealous fans occasionally take things too far. One year, an Ohio State fan physically attacked someone simply because they wore Michigan colors outside the stadium, forgetting that they're both humans who enjoy cheering for their favorite team.

To varying degrees, countless sports fans around the world have experienced similar feelings of intensity and euphoria. When our favorite team wins, we yell, "We won!!" even though *we* never stepped foot on the field. Fans relish the honor that comes with associating with winners. This same feeling is why we name-drop. It also fuels the competitive spirit to prove that *our* group is better than *their* group.

Similarly, the Corinthians were professional honor chasers. They knew how to play the game. But they didn't seem to know what team they belonged to. The Corinthian believers formed factions around the person who baptized them (1 Cor. 1:12–15). Why all the clamoring to identify with one or another person? Who we are, partly depends on the people with whom we associate. Our identity reflects our sense of worth and what we value. But the Corinthians grasped something that we sometimes forget— we first know *whose we are* and only then know *who we are*.

We belong to a king who emptied himself upon a cross, enduring its shame. This fact changes our identity. Our essential identity isn't determined by our network, education, or job title. We do not define ourselves fundamentally as "wise," "strong," "Jew," or "Greek" (1:20, 24). Paul challenges the zeal to boast in those distinctions that push us to compete with one another. In 1 Corinthians 1:26–29, he says:

> *Consider your own call, brothers, and sisters: not many of you were wise by human standards, not many were powerful, and not many were of noble birth. But God chose what is foolish in the world to shame the wise; God chose what is weak in the world to shame the strong; God chose what is low and despised in the world, things that are not, to reduce to nothing things that are, so that no one might boast in the presence of God.*

Deep down, what makes you feel important? Being better than others in some aspect of life? Or belonging to Christ?

Parting Reflection

Read 1 Corinthians 1:10–31. Identify ways that you have acted like the Corinthians in this passage. How might you counteract any competitive tendencies within your church community?

Parting Prayer

Father, we are one people, one family. Competition and comparison should have no place among us. In love, discipline us where we need correction and training. Purify our hearts so that all glory goes to you. Thank you for the oneness that we share in Christ.

Do All to the Glory of God

────────── ⑇ ──────────

So, whether you eat or drink, or whatever you do, do everything for the glory of God.

—1 COR. 10:31

First Corinthians 10:31 is well known among many Christians. For some, it is a life verse because, as one Bible commentator said, "Every aspect of every Christian's life has the potential to honor God."[75] In fact, John Piper once wrote an article titled "How to Drink Orange Juice to the Glory of God." He pointed out that believers could honor God even in mundane tasks like drinking orange juice by first recognizing that "the juice, and even our strength to drink it, is a free gift of God."[76] A proper response to such a reality should be to drink with a truly thankful heart toward God, with which we glorify God as we enjoy our morning beverage. While this is a good insight and a disposition we should consider, there is also a communal aspect of doing all to the glory of God that is present in 1 Corinthians.

In 1 Corinthians 8 and 10:1–22, Paul deals with eating food offered to idols in pagan temples. A key principle for Christians in such situations is that while it is true that "no idol in the world really exists" (8:4), we should be mindful of how our knowledge and actions impact the faith of others. We may know that God has no law against a certain action, but if we flaunt that in front of less mature Christians who don't possess the same knowledge, we

───────────────

75. Frank S. Thielman contributed to the ESV Study Bible by providing the study notes for 1 Corinthians. This quote comes from his commentary on 1 Corinthians 10:31. *The ESV Study Bible, English Standard Version* (Wheaton, IL: Crossway Books, 2008).
76. John Piper, *How to Drink Orange Juice to the Glory of God*, https://www.desiringgod.org /articles/how-to-drink-orange-juice-to-the-glory-of-god.

may damage their faith. So, Paul concludes, "If what I eat causes my brother or sister to fall into sin, I will never eat meat again" (8:13 NIV).

Paul then extends this principle in 10:23–11:1 and says, "Do not seek your own advantage, but that of the other" (10:24). He then brings up a hypothetical situation where a person receives food and is told that it was offered in a sacrifice. Paul already made clear that before God there is nothing wrong with eating such food; however, he says, "Do not eat it, for the sake of the one who informed you, and for the sake of conscience—I do not mean your conscience, but his" (10:28–29). In other words, communal harmony is more important than our individual liberties. It is here that 1 Corinthians 10:31(quoted above) comes as a conclusion to the preceding arguments.

When Paul mentions eating and drinking in 10:31, he almost certainly isn't thinking about honoring God by simply drinking a beverage or having a snack. Instead, he has in mind what he had discussed in chapters 8 and 10.[77] Thus, a primary way that we "do everything for the glory of God" is by seeking the good of others ahead of our own with a mind's eye toward their salvation and growth in the faith. We very well may have individual rights or liberties, but for the sake of the gospel, we must not allow those to trump harmony within the community.

Parting Reflection

What is the first thing that comes to your mind when thinking about how to apply 1 Corinthians 10:31? Have you ever considered that a primary way to fulfill this command is by looking outward to others (and our actions toward them) instead of an inward attitude toward certain tasks?

Parting Prayer

Lord, we confess that too often we act in ways that do not honor you, whether it's taking a harsh tone toward others or ignoring their spiritual well-being. Spirit, help us to be more aware of how we honor or dishonor you with our actions toward others. Help us to seek our neighbor's good ahead of our own.

---

77. The third paragraph discusses how Paul addressed food. Drinking is specifically addressed in 1 Cor. 10:21.

Veiling as a Matter of Status

———————— ⑈ ————————

However, in the Lord, neither is woman independent of man, nor is man independent of woman. For as the woman originates from the man, so also the man has his birth through the woman; and all things originate from God.

—1 COR. 11:11–12

First Corinthians 11 is a notoriously confounding chapter, particularly in regard to veiling and what Paul means by it. Some readers assume Paul orders Corinthian women to veil their hair because they effectively are stubborn feminists who want to express their individuality or even sexuality. But what if it's the men, not the women, who are the target of Paul's rebuke? And what if a key issue in this chapter has to do with status?

Paul frequently quotes and then corrects the Corinthians with his letter. He appears to do so again here, quoting the Corinthians in 11:4–5, 7–10.[78] The status-driven Corinthians misunderstand Paul's teaching about headship and so compel women to wear a veil. The extreme penalty in verse 6 (cutting off one's hair) shows the absurdity of the Corinthian's ideas expressed in 11:4–5. They defend this symbolic subjugation in 11:7–10 using a distorted reading of Genesis. In 11:11–12, Paul sets them right, explaining that men and women are interdependent. Regardless of the order in which God created man and woman, both depend on the other and originate from God.

Verse 13 asks rhetorically, "Is it proper for a woman to pray to God with her head uncovered?" Yes, it is! Paul exposes their contradictory thinking,

---

78. For a fuller explanation, see Lucy Peppiatt, *Women and Worship in Corinth* (Eugene, OR: Cascade Books, 2015), which is summarized in a popular version *Unveiling Paul's Women: Making Sense of 1 Corinthians 11:2–16* (Eugene, OR: Cascade Books, 2018). Paul quotes in 1 Corinthians 1:12; 3:4; 6:12–13; 7:1; 8:1, 4, 8; 10:23. Possible instances are 4:6b; 8:5a; 12:3; 15:12, 35.

saying something like this: "You guys already recognize that long hair acts like a covering (11:4, 14), which is why you think men are dishonorable with long hair. However, you don't apply this same logic to women. The woman's *glorious* hair serves as a cover, yet you, Corinthians, want her to cover that glory."

Paul engages in a theological argument, not merely a cultural one. Moreover, 11:16 makes clear that his message applies beyond the situation in Corinth. Paul does not compel women to wear veils in all the churches (1 Tim. 2:9). Instead, he solves a cultural problem concerning status by correcting the Corinthians' mistaken interpretation and application of Genesis. It is Paul who wants to liberate the Corinthian women, throwing off the veil of subordination and raising them up to their God-given equal status with men.

Parting Reflection

How might you or your church unwittingly make some people feel marginalized or like second-class citizens? How might women around you not feel honored or valued?

Parting Prayer

Father, you have made us your sons and daughters. Grant us eyes that are not biased by cultural assumptions that minimize others' value. May we genuinely honor one another as your children.

Paul's Motive for Ministry

———— ·⫼⫼· ————

When I came to Troas to proclaim the good news of Christ, a door
was opened for me in the Lord; but my mind could not rest because
I did not find my brother Titus there. So I said farewell to them and
went on to Macedonia.

—2 COR. 2:12–13

What motivates missionaries? Several things, of course, like the salvation of unreached peoples and the desire to glorify God. Still, Paul hints at a fundamental motivation in Romans and 2 Corinthians that we often overlook. Although Paul says, "A door was opened for me in the Lord," he passes up that opportunity for fruitful ministry. Why!? Paul is simply too concerned for Titus and the well-being of the Corinthian church to continue through that open door. He seems to do something similar in Romans, where he delays a missionary journey to Spain to deliver aid to the Jerusalem church.

What lies beneath Paul's anxiety? Above all, Paul wants God's approval or commendation.[79] He also pursues "glory and honor and immortality" on the day of judgment (Rom. 2:6–11, 29). In fact, Jesus himself urges his disciples to seek reward (Matt. 5:11–12; Mark 9:41). And along with all of God's people, Paul longs to be called "good and faithful" (Matt. 25:21).

How do these desires relate to his actions in 2 Corinthians and Romans? Paul is concerned that his ministry produces *lasting* fruit. Elliot Clark observes:

> In missions, we recruit missionaries with urgency, not toward longevity. . . .
> While our missionary mantra of late has been "Work yourself out of a job,"

———————————

79. Compare 1 Corinthians 3:14–15; 9:24–27; 2 Corinthians 5:9–10; 2 Timothy 2:15. For a fuller explanation, see Elliot Clark, *Mission Affirmed: Recovering the Missionary Motivation of Paul* (Wheaton, IL: Crossway, 2022).

one has to wonder if a more appropriate goal would be, "Build something that lasts." . . . Paul connected his boasting to the strength, stability, and long-term viability of a congregation.[80]

Paul is determined that his ministry labor is not done in vain. He tells the Philippians, "It is by your holding fast to the word of life that I can boast on the day of Christ that I did not run in vain or labor in vain" (Phil. 2:16; cf. 1 Thess. 3:5). Sadly, he tells the Galatians, "I am afraid that my work for you may have been wasted" (Gal. 4:11).

Faithful gospel ministry is a long-term, relationally intensive labor of love. While people around us applaud rapid results and quick methods, these are not the basis of God's approval. Fruitfulness involves more than having large numbers of attendees and converts. Instead, the fruit of the Spirit is Christlike character.

Parting Reflection

Why might God not approve of one's ministry even if it has many participants? In your life and ministry, what kind of fruitfulness do you seek in practice?

Parting Prayer

God, we long to please you and not labor in vain. Strengthen us in the face of temptations to compromise. You are the only source of genuine Spiritual fruit.

---

80. Elliot Clark, *Mission Affirmed*, 21, 53.

Looking to Eternal Honor

───────────── ⫸⫷ ─────────────

For this slight momentary affliction is preparing us for an eternal
weight of glory beyond all measure, because we look not at what can
be seen but at what cannot be seen; for what can be seen is temporary,
but what cannot be seen is eternal.

—2 COR. 4:17–18

Nobody wants to suffer. We know it is inevitable, be it our own or the agony we witness a loved one go through. No one wants to, but we must. Given its certainty, the bigger question is how we will deal with suffering. One reason the Bible is wonderful is that it gives us true answers to life's deepest questions, just like this one. In 2 Corinthians 4, Paul embraces the fact that even we who are in Christ are like jars of clay (4:7). But we don't lose courage. We aren't defeated because "even though our outer nature is wasting away, our inner nature is being renewed day by day" (4:16). Paul elaborates in verses 17–18 (quoted above).

First, any suffering that we experience is a "slight momentary affliction." Now, of course, "momentary" doesn't mean that it won't last a long time, and "slight" doesn't mean it won't be painful. Recall the woman "who had been suffering from hemorrhages for twelve years; and though she had spent all she had on physicians, no one could cure her" (Luke 8:43). Twelve years of suffering! If we could talk to her at that time, she wouldn't have said that her suffering and shame were slight and momentary. But if we could talk to her now, nearly 2,000 years later and with an eternity at Christ's side ahead of her, she would undoubtedly say that her earthly suffering was a "slight momentary affliction." So, we must view our suffering from an eternal perspective.

Next, as we patiently endure suffering, it is "preparing us for an eternal weight of glory beyond all measure." As we persevere in our outer self, we renew our inner self as we seek God's face and recall his "extraordinary power" by which he "who raised the Lord Jesus will raise us" (2 Cor. 4:7, 14). And when we are raised, we'll be given new and glorified bodies (5:1–5). Therefore, must understand that what awaits us is both eternal and glorious beyond compare.

Last of all, we actualize this confidence by looking "not at what can be seen but at what cannot be seen." This means that we must not fixate attention on our trials here and now. We don't ignore our present agony, but we certainly don't let it consume us. Instead, we live knowing that suffering's temporary nature is overshadowed by the eternal glory that God has for us. And this is certain because "he who has prepared us for this very thing is God, who has given us the Spirit as a guarantee" (5:5).

Parting Reflection

What does it mean to say that God will honor us by giving us glorified bodies? What else about heaven shows the honor that God will bestow on us? How should we respond?

Parting Prayer

Lord, help us to be of good courage as we make it our aim to please you in all that we do. Help us to walk by faith, not by sight.

Christian Boasting

——————— ⼋⼁⼁⼁⼁⼋ ———————

But if I wish to boast, I will not be a fool, for I will be speaking the truth.
But I refrain from it, so that no one may think better of me than what
is seen in me or heard from me.

—2 COR. 12:6

I once attended a church where a pastor was particularly boastful of his accomplishments. He had completed a doctorate and made sure that the prefix "Dr." went before his name when in print. Occasionally, he'd even remind everyone that he was a doctor while preaching. Have you ever met someone like this?

People typically boast about themselves because they want the honor and respect that they feel is due to them. Perhaps they worked very hard to get to where they are or have gone through rigorous experiences. Regardless, they want to be recognized for it. This is understandable but, as Christians, should we boast of our accomplishments?

In Corinth, a group of "super-apostles" shows up looking to smear Paul's reputation. This results in him feeling compelled to defend the merit of his ministry, which he does at length in 2 Corinthians 10–12. It shouldn't be too difficult. After all, the risen Jesus appeared to him (Acts 9), and his list of missionary accomplishments is second to none (2 Cor. 11:21–28). Yet, the discomfort and unnaturalness Paul feels about boasting of his accomplishments ooze from the text. "I wish you would bear with me in a little foolishness . . . I am talking like a madman" (2 Cor. 11:1, 23). Paul concludes about boasting in his ministry, "I have been a fool! You forced me to it" (2 Cor. 12:11).

During Paul's discourse, two principles of boasting are apparent. First, our boasting should not be to get recognition for ourselves, but in that which demonstrates God's work in our lives. Paul states, "If I must boast, I will boast of the things that show my weakness" (11:30). Then, in chapter 12, he speaks of his vision of paradise and the resulting thorn in his flesh. It is in this context that verse 6 (quoted above) appears. Paul would be telling the truth if he boasted about this incredible vision, yet he refrains from it, so others won't make much of him. Why? Because he wants others to make much of Christ instead. "So, I will boast all the more gladly of my weaknesses, so that the power of Christ may dwell in me" (2 Cor. 12:9b). Second, we should not boast about our personal accomplishments; instead, we should boast that we know the Lord. In 2 Corinthians 10:17–18, Paul alludes to Jeremiah 9:23–24 when he says, "'Let the one who boasts, boast in the Lord.' For it is not those who commend themselves that are approved, but those whom the Lord commends." So, let us not be concerned with commending ourselves to others. Rather, let us rest in the truth that God has reconciled us to himself.

Parting Reflection

Read Jeremiah 9:23–24. In what ways have you boasted (whether verbally or nonverbally) to others about your wisdom, power, or riches? How can you boast to others about understanding and knowing the Lord?

Parting Prayer

Lord, forgive us for being far too concerned with what others think about us. We know that in the grand scheme of things, their commendation does not matter. Help us to remember and to see the ways that your power rests on us, then may we boast in that.

The Antidote to People-Pleasing

Am I now seeking human approval, or God's approval? Or am I trying to please people? If I were still pleasing people, I would not be a servant of Christ.

—GAL. 1:10

I vividly remember talking with an old friend, debating whether to tell him something. It was an announcement of a significant accomplishment, but a premature one because it wasn't yet official. Alas, I blurted it out. For whatever reason, I've long felt a need for this friend's approval. When around him, I tend to act in ways or say things I otherwise wouldn't. My wife recognized this and astutely asked, "Why do you care so much what he thinks?" In many respects, seeking the approval of others is a vain and dangerous game. Worse yet, it can contaminate our character if we're not careful.

Paul illustrates the dangers of people-pleasing when he recalls his interaction with Peter in Antioch (Gal. 2:11–14). Peter had freely associated with both Jews and Gentiles, but when "certain men from James came," Peter "drew back and kept himself separate for fear of the circumcision faction" (2:12). Peter's actions no doubt left the Gentile Christians feeling inferior. Worse yet, his actions influenced other Jewish Christians to act hypocritically, notably Barnabas. This behavior led Paul to sharply rebuke Peter in front of everyone, which likely shamed Peter. So, how can we avoid being led into undesirable situations by our desire to please others?

In Galatians 1:10 (quoted above), Paul offers an antidote to people-pleasing: Being a servant of Christ should supersede the fleshly desire to please man. What does this mean? It's not that seeking the approval of others is always wrong; instead, it must be filtered through the lens of being a servant of Christ and thus being chiefly concerned with pleasing God. Elsewhere, Paul says:

> *It is a very small thing that I should be judged by you or by any human court.*
> *I do not even judge myself. I am not aware of anything against myself, but I*
> *am not thereby acquitted. It is the Lord who judges me.*
> —1 Cor. 4:3–4

The antidote is not a brazen, devil-may-care attitude. Instead, it is to be so deeply rooted in and satisfied with God's acceptance of us that the opinions of others do not enslave us.

At that moment with my friend, I lacked contentment in God's approval of me through Christ. This led me to blurt out my accomplishment prematurely to (hopefully) get my friend's approval. In short, I was seeking the approval of others. While my misstep wasn't as consequential as Peter's, it highlights just how easily we are led off course by people-pleasing. If we're not careful, we quickly slip into acting in ways or saying things that we otherwise never would.

Parting Reflection

How have you valued others' approval over God's approval of you? Around certain people, do you slip into acting in ways or saying things you otherwise wouldn't? If so, why do you think that is?

Parting Prayer

Lord, we confess that we are too often concerned with pleasing others above our desire to please you. Help us to find rest in you. Turn the words of the well-known hymn into reality for us:

> *Riches I heed not, nor vain, empty praise*
> *Thou mine inheritance, now and always*
> *Thou and thou only first in my heart*
> *High King of heaven, my treasure thou art*

When It's Good to Be Made Much Of

———————— ·⫴⫼⫴· ————————

They make much of you, but for no good purpose; they want to exclude you, so that you may make much of them. It is good to be made much of for a good purpose at all times, and not only when I am present with you.

—GAL. 4:17–18

My youngest son sat on the couch brushing my wife's hair. He looked up and randomly told her she was a beautiful princess. Now, she was on to him. "Ok, what do you want?" she laughed. He couldn't contain his smirk, knowing his plan was foiled. From an early age, our son learned that intentional praise and affection could go a long way in helping him to get what he wanted. But we knew how he worked.

By contrast, the Galatians were oblivious to the schemes of false teachers. While Paul was physically absent, these teachers used flattery to form a wedge between Paul and the churches of Galatia. He exposed the dangers they faced by tolerating a false gospel (Gal. 1:6–9). For Paul, love meant "telling [them] the truth" (4:16). He does not use praise to curry favor for himself. Instead, like a mother, he labored so that Christ would be formed in them (4:19). Still, the Galatians treated him like an enemy! Who rejects the one who gave them life? What shame!

While applause and agreement are forms of encouragement, they can also be manipulation. That kind of praise can lower our defenses and keep us from being sober-minded. We come to equate love with being made much of. We gather friends and follow people on social media who tell us that we're OK, good, and even exceptional. Yet, when they praise us, they merely applaud their own beliefs and behaviors. After all, if they criticize us, they would simply be highlighting their own errors.

Paul is correct, "It is good to be made much of," but only if we live in a manner worthy of respect and honor. While we don't want to be paranoid, we should examine the praise we receive from others in order to determine if it is truly "for a good purpose." On the other side, we must never use flattery to manipulate others; instead, we should be quick to praise others as they glorify Christ. Likewise, we need to ask ourselves, "Who has loved me by speaking the truth? Have I overlooked these people because I confuse love with being praised?"

Parting Reflection

Spend time in prayer and reflection, considering the question above, "Who has loved me by speaking the truth? Have I overlooked these people because I confuse love with being praised?" How might you need to respond in light of your answers?

Parting Prayer

Thank you, Lord, for always speaking the truth in love and for sending others in our life who do the same. Spirit, grant us wisdom to discern when we might behave like those Galatians, using honor as a way of manipulating people rather than loving them. You are the God of all truth.

Grace for the Unworthy

——————— ⑉ ———————

For by grace you have been saved through faith, and this is not your own doing; it is the gift of God.

—EPH. 2:8

The Greek word that we translate "grace" simply means "gift." Giving gifts or doing favors is an essential aspect of social life. However, its significance differs across time and place. Historically and in many cultures today, grace does not refer to a gift with no strings attached. In other words, grace is given *with* an expectation of return. In fact, that notion of grace was largely foreign to ancient thinkers.[81]

There are two aspects of grace that modern Westerners often insufficiently understand. First, gift-giving is an integral part of *creating and strengthening relationships.* Gifts can express solidarity, celebration, or concern. Therefore, relationships marked by love seek to deepen mutual bonds of indebtedness. In that sense, grace without an expectation of mutual reciprocity is simply not grace. Consequently, anyone who did not respond to a gift by appropriately reciprocating would be deemed dishonorable and ungrateful.

A second feature characterized grace in the Greco-Roman world. A person didn't haphazardly offer gifts (i.e., grace). Since gifts knit people together, one was careful to only be generous with someone the giver regarded as worthy. By analogy, consider why you might donate money to a charity? It's not because they "earn" it in the same way employees have a legal right to receive pay from employers. Instead, we give to organizations that we feel do meaningful work in responsible ways. In that sense, we choose to give to *worthy* charities. Our gifts then reflect the honor we bestow on them.

---

81. John Barclay, *Paul and the Gift* (Grand Rapids, MI: Eerdmans, 2015), 498.

These dynamics illuminate Paul's message. God graciously gives the Law to ancient Israel, establishing a unique relationship with them. Therefore, many Israelites assumed that following their ancestral traditions marked them as *worthy* of God's salvation. However, Christ removes the standard criteria of worth, like wealth, ethnicity, and gender. New Testament scholar, John Barclay, describes those who follow Christ when he says:

> God pays no regard to the "face" (Gal 2:6) but distributes his grace without regard for the worth. . . . The [church] forms a new community of opinion, constituted by the gift to the unworthy. Within this community arises, of course, an alternative system of worth, a new form of "symbolic capital."[82]

No wonder Paul says to the Corinthians, "Everything is for your sake, so that grace, as it extends to more and more people, *may increase thanksgiving, to the glory of God*" (2 Cor. 4:15 emphasis added).

Parting Reflection

While you might not think you can "earn" salvation, how might you sometimes think of yourself as worthy of God's grace? You might want to see Colossians 1:10 or 1 Thessalonians 2:12. How can you appropriately and practically respond to his grace?

Parting Prayer

Father, you love us who are unworthy. You even adopt us as children to the praise of your glorious grace that you freely bestowed on us in the Beloved (Eph. 1:6). Renew our minds, Holy Spirit, that we might live for the praise of your glory because we better perceive the treasures of Christ's grace.

---

82. Barclay, 435.

Salvation As Group Membership

—————————— ·⫼⫼⫼· ——————————

So then you are no longer strangers and aliens, but you are citizens
with the saints and also members of the household of God.

—EPH. 2:19

In Scripture, salvation is intertwined with group membership. The church
is a community for all who call on Jesus as Lord, regardless of one's social
status. Those who are considered great in the world have the same inheritance and standing as those that are "outsiders" by the standards of the age.
God bestows honor to each member of his family through the blood of Jesus.
This reality transcends all other perceived barriers between people, which
prompts Paul to write:

> *There is no longer Jew or Greek, there is no longer slave or free, there is no*
> *longer male and female; for all of you are one in Christ Jesus. And if you belong*
> *to Christ, then you are Abraham's offspring, heirs according to the promise.*
> —Gal. 3:28–29

Jayson Georges and Mark Baker go so far as to say that this "new group
status *is* salvation itself."[83] Belonging to God's family brings salvation in several ways, but one example is this: it saves us from putting an undue value
on our social status or family lineage. In another letter, Paul considers his
vaunted family lineage within Jewish culture "as rubbish in order that I may
gain Christ" (Phil. 3:8). In other words, in light of belonging to the household
of God, Paul views his previous family heritage as worthless. His sense of
value is now found in belonging to God and being a member of his family.

---

83. Georges and Baker, *Ministering in Honor-Shame Cultures*, 178.

While Paul was born into an honorable social status, many in this world aren't so fortunate. In all likelihood, the vast majority of humans come from less-than-honorable backgrounds. For those on the margins of society, their social status can leave them in disrepute. Georges and Baker explain that:

> The honor derived from joining God's prestigious family is good news for people afflicted by shame. Regardless of what false social mechanisms of exclusion they fall victim to, those in Christ are eternally honored and accepted as members in the people of God, with full rights, privileges, and status.[84]

And this is precisely what Paul has in mind in Ephesians 2:11–22 (partially quoted above). Christ has united all—even strangers and aliens—into the family of God through his shed blood. Jesus grants equal access for all to the Spirit. Christ is the cornerstone, and all of us who believe in Christ are "being built together into a dwelling place for God by the Spirit" (2:22 ESV).

Parting Reflection

Do you tend to view your salvation primarily from an individualistic perspective? While our salvation is valid, how does the reality of salvation as group membership inform your faith?

Parting Prayer

Lord, we thank you for including us in your family and bestowing upon us all the honor, rights, and privileges that come with being your children. Give us eyes to see what may be missing in our thought processes about our membership in this family.

---

84. Georges and Baker, 178.

Overturning Gender Stereotypes

———— ⫶⫶⫶⫶ ————

Husbands, love your wives, just as Christ loved the church and gave himself up for her, in order to make her holy by cleansing her with the washing of water by the word.

—EPH. 5:25–26

Many weddings recall Paul's famous words in Ephesians 5, where he addresses the relationship between Christian husbands and wives. What people often don't realize is just how revolutionary this passage was for his time. Today, readers frequently focus on how wives should be "subject" to their husbands and that husbands should "love your wives, just as Christ loved the church." Yet, this emphasis only gives us a small glimpse into what Paul is doing. In fact, his words would have sounded thoroughly offensive to many men of his day.

In the first century, women were treated with less honor than men, as if second-class citizens. Regularly denied an education, women were subject to the dictates of their fathers or husbands. Ancient men even thanked God that he had not made them to be women! While this view is foreign, even repugnant, to us today, many contemporary interpreters still seem to use Ephesians 5 in a way that honors husbands at the expense of their wives. They emphasize, "the husband is the head of the wife just as Christ is the head of the church, the body of which he is the Savior" (5:23) while never grasping the subversive spirit of Paul's message.

Paul beckons husbands to act like women and slaves. The responsibilities of women and slaves overlapped much. They oversaw making clothes, preparing food, tending children, and taking care of laundry. Similarly, in Ephesians 5, Paul assigns the husband with tasks that would normally be considered domestic tasks or "women's work." "[T]he husband is directed to serve his wife by doing low-status work typical of women and slaves."[85] Husbands should wash their wives by the word, presenting her without spots or wrinkles. They must "nourish and tenderly care" for her. According to Paul's imagery, what (or *who*) counts as the husband's own body? His wife! Being one flesh with her, he, metaphorically speaking, has a woman's body.

Ephesians 5 reverses standard expectations of hierarchy and status. In fact, similar "household codes" existed in the ancient world, but Paul uniquely addresses his comments to people deemed lower by ordinary social sensibilities. In this way, Paul honors the marginalized and humbles the privileged.

Parting Reflection

Have you ever witnessed or participated in unhealthy relationships between men and women, husbands and wives? What is Christ's countercultural challenge to those relationships?

Parting Prayer

We rejoice that "there is no longer male and female . . . in Christ" (Gal. 3:28). Spirit, guide us into repentance so that we might have a right view of the opposite gender and bring healing where there have been hurts. Thank you for your word that washes over us.

---

85. Cynthia Long Westfall, *Paul and Gender: Reclaiming the Apostle's Vision for Men and Women in Christ* (Grand Rapids, MI: Baker, 2016), 23, 101–102.

Working for the Glory of Others

———————— ·‖‖‖· ————————

Do nothing from selfish ambition or conceit but in humility regard others as better than yourselves.

—PHIL. 2:3

Similar to today, Christians in the first century also struggled to get along. To no one's surprise, then, unity is a primary emphasis in Paul's letter to the Philippians. At the start of chapter two, he pleads with them, essentially saying, "If you're claiming to be a Christian, then act like it!" Now, of course, Paul was more articulate and gentler, but that's the gist of his meaning. So, how can we act as followers of Christ and have unity with each other?

Paul lays out a two-step process. Negatively, we shouldn't act selfishly by looking only at our own interests. Positively, we should consider others more honorable than ourselves, looking first to their interests (2:3–4).[86] Paul then shows how Christ embodied this mindset in his life, death, and resurrection in the beautiful words of 2:5–11.

Similarly, a primary aim for ministers of the gospel is to serve so that people may receive glory. Practically, this can be done by actively looking to give honor to others. Jesus did this regularly. In Mark 2:15–17, he gives honor to the tax collectors and sinners by being a guest in their house. This draws the ire of the Pharisees, which leads them to malign Jesus's name. Elsewhere, Paul concludes an explanation of his ministry by saying that he suffers in part

---

86. Inherent in regarding "others as better than yourselves" is showing honor to them. The New Testament authors regularly exhort their readers to express such a disposition. See Romans 12:10; 1 Timothy 5:17; 1 Peter 2:17.

for the glory of others (Eph. 3:13). Finally, serving so that others may receive glory also means shielding them from shame.[87]

Such a lifestyle of service is natural to Christ because such a mindset reflects the essence of who he is. However, we too are in Christ and have his Spirit inside us. And while it's warranted to look at Christ's activity as an example for us to follow, there is something deeper for us to understand. Our motivation shouldn't simply be to follow Jesus's ethical model. It is not, "Act like Christ and then we'll be his follower." Instead, our impetus for serving others is our union with Christ. We belong to him, baptized into his death and resurrection. Jesus gave his life to reconcile us to God. In doing so, he unites us to himself, and our only proper response is to serve others as he served us. In other words, "We *are* in Christ, so now we must act like it." This is our deepest desire, thanks to the Spirit. If he sought to honor others, then so shall we. And as we increasingly look to serve others, unity is sure to follow.

Parting Reflection

What's the difference between "Act like Christ and then we'll be his follower" and "We are in Christ, so now we must act like it"? Can you think of other ways that Jesus honors others? How can you live out your union with Christ by doing the same?

Parting Prayer

Spirit, make us realize that we are truly in Christ and all that entails for us. Instead of mere outward attempts at holiness, may we release a love for holiness, gifted to us by the Spirit. Orient our hearts so that we might joyfully serve for the sake of your glory and the honor of all people.

---

87. See the entry in John 2:9–10 where Jesus protects the bridegroom's family from shame by turning water into wine.

Responding to Reconciliation

———————— ·⫼· ————————

If indeed you continue in the faith, stable and steadfast, not shifting
from the hope of the gospel that you heard.

—COL. 1:23 ESV

In this book's introduction and our entry on Ephesians 2:8, we note that reciprocity is a critical concept in collectivist cultures. Exchanging favors and gifts creates and sustains relationships. It ensures harmony. Not reciprocating favors would break from social expectations and be deemed shameful. Instead, when a gift is offered and accepted, the receiving party is expected to respond accordingly.

This concept is clear in Paul's letter to the Colossians. Paul first exalts in the preeminence of Christ and how, through Jesus, God was pleased to "reconcile to himself all things, whether on earth or in heaven, by making peace through the blood of his cross" (1:20). He then describes the status reversal that God works for Christians. Believers in Christ were once alienated from God but are now set apart for God (i.e., made holy). We go from being hostile in mind to being blameless, and from doing evil deeds to being above reproach (1:21–22). This harkens back to 1:13–14, where Paul says the Father has "rescued us from the power of darkness and transferred us into the kingdom of his beloved Son, in whom we have redemption, the forgiveness of sins." God truly does a tremendous work for us and gives us a breathtaking gift.

As such, Paul presumes that we will reciprocate by continuing "in the faith, stable and steadfast, not shifting from the hope of the gospel that [we] heard" (1:23 ESV). The apostle is saying that we should respond to God's gift of reconciliation by trusting in him and holding fast to what the Bible teaches us. By doing so, we honor God, and our relationship with him is strengthened. In other words, our good deeds are not simply something we do to demonstrate or provide evidence for a transformed life. Instead, they are the fitting response to God's gift of reconciliation and show that we truly value the relationship.

Parting Reflection

Colossians 1:10 says that if we walk in a manner worthy of the Lord, it pleases God. With the idea of reciprocity in mind, why might this be pleasing to God? What are we signaling to him when we walk in a worthy manner?

Parting Prayer

Let's pray Paul's prayer in Colossians 1:9–10, asking God that we may be:

> *Filled with the knowledge of God's will in all spiritual wisdom and understanding, so that [we] may lead lives worthy of the Lord, fully pleasing to him, as [we] bear fruit in every good work and as [we] grow in the knowledge of God.*

Justification and Ascribed Honor

———————— ⦿ ————————

If anyone else has reason to be confident in the flesh, I have more.

—PHIL. 3:4B

The President of China does not wake up each morning asking, "How will a holy God accept me, a sinner?" He doesn't have Martin Luther's angst wondering whether he has done enough to merit God's favor. As the leader of the Chinese Communist Party, he is an atheist and far more concerned with maintaining a strong network of relationships. Like countless other Chinese, he cares about his social status, position, and "face." In this way, Paul might understand the Chinese President better than Western Christians.

When sharing the gospel, many missionaries presume Chinese people have a mindset that is far more characteristic of Western Christendom. In short, they suppose that the Chinese are primarily concerned with doing enough good works to earn their way to heaven. While Chinese people certainly care about morality, they're not driven by this theological view so common in the West. Their thinking more closely resembles that seen in Philippians 3. Teachers often use this chapter to emphasize the point that no one is justified (i.e., declared right) through good moral works. However, this interpretation overlooks much of Paul's argument.

Paul denounces "a righteousness of my own that comes from the law" (3:9). But how does he do so? He says, "If anyone else has reason to be confident in the flesh, I have more: circumcised on the eighth day, a member of the people of Israel, of the tribe of Benjamin, a Hebrew born of Hebrews; as to the law, a Pharisee" (3:4–5). Paul mentions circumcision, lineage, and position. Each is an example of *ascribed honor*. They mark him as a "Hebrew of Hebrews." It's only in verse 6 that Paul mentions anything that could be interpreted as *achieved honor*. He says, "as to zeal, a persecutor of the church; as to righteousness under the law, blameless." While Paul's identity includes both ascribed and achieved honor, he predominantly emphasizes the former.

The Law of Moses distinguishes Jews from gentiles. Israel felt having God's Law set them apart as holy, and worthy of unique honor among the nations. Yet, Paul disputes such criteria of worth and therefore justification. The truly justified are those "who worship in the Spirit of God and boast in Christ Jesus" (3:3). As John Barclay explains, justification is not a precondition of salvation; instead, it's the declaration that "the saving gift has already been given in Christ, without regard to worth."[88] And not just *achieved* worth but also *ascribed* worth.

Parting Reflection

What makes you feel like you are "enough" or worthy of people's acceptance? How do you seek ascribed honor?

Parting Prayer

Father, you sent Christ without regard for our worth, as commonly defined by our community. It is your Son alone who deserves ultimate praise (Phil. 2:9–11). Thank you that we are ascribed honor in Christ because of the unique honor that he achieves.

_____

88. Barclay, *Paul, and the Gift*, 378.

Vessels for Honorable Use

───────── ·⫸⫷· ─────────

Therefore, if anyone cleanses himself from what is dishonorable, he will be a vessel for honorable use, set apart as holy, useful to the master of the house, ready for every good work.

—2 TIM. 2:21 ESV

Second Timothy 2:14–26 offers a contrast between Timothy as a faithful minister of the gospel and the false teachers. Paul urges Timothy, "Do your best to present yourself to God as one approved by him, a worker who has no need to be ashamed, rightly explaining the word of truth" (2:15). This verse provides a hint at how Timothy—and us by extension—can be workers who have no need to be ashamed. First, we should primarily seek God's approval, not that of other people. As the entry on Matthew 6:5–6 discussed, how we pursue honor and whom we seek approval from matters. Second, the doctrine is important. Paul mentions two contemptible individuals, Hymenaeus and Philetus, who upset the faith of some believers. How did they do this? With doctrine—they taught that the resurrection had already happened. Their doctrine was not healthy or sound; instead, Paul described it as being like "gangrene," which can dangerously spread (2:17).

In 2:20–21, Paul uses an illustration to explain his point. A "large house" is worthy of honor, yet inside there are vessels for honorable use ("gold and silver") and dishonorable use ("wood and clay"). Naturally, the vessels for honorable use are more desirable and "useful to the owner of the house." As Paul suggests, we should seek to cleanse ourselves "from what is dishonorable" so that we will be "a vessel for honorable use." But how?

Dishonorable vessels are so doctrinally and morally. A doctrinal example was given above with Hymenaeus and Philetus. Morally, we are dishonorable to God when we indulge in "youthful passions," partake in "senseless con-troversies," and are "quarrelsome" (2:22–24). Conversely, we can be vessels for honorable use in two ways. Doctrinally, we can honor God as we "rightly

196

handle the word of truth" (2:15 ESV) Our teaching should not "breed quarrels" or "lead people into more and more ungodliness" (2:14, 16 ESV). Instead, it should point others to a knowledge of the truth. Morally, we should "depart from iniquity" and "cleanse [ourselves] from what is dishonorable" (2:19, 21 ESV).

Just as vessels of gold and silver give honor to the owner of a great house, so we give honor to God through having sound doctrine and living it out with vigilance as we "pursue righteousness, faith, love, and peace, along with those who call on the Lord from a pure heart" (2:22).

Parting Reflection

Have you ever considered that your doctrine can bring either honor or dishonor to God? How have you witnessed Christians dishonor God with their doctrine? In what ways have you dishonored God with your doctrine?

Parting Prayer

Father, we take rest in knowing that you know those who are yours and that you have called us to yourself through Christ. We confess that we often fail to honor you both morally and with our doctrine. We agree and love the trustworthy saying, "If we are faithless, he remains faithful." We confess our faithlessness and praise you that you remain faithful.

Let Marriage Be Held in Honor

⫘

Let marriage be held in honor by all, and let the marriage bed be kept undefiled; for God will judge fornicators and adulterers.

—HEB. 13:4

What does it mean to hold marriage in honor? To start, we must understand that marriage was instituted by God at creation. It is foundational to human society. That is not to say that every person must get married. After all, Jesus himself did not marry in his earthly life. The point is that marriage is not a human creation. Instead, it was made by God for the good of society. Above that, we must also understand that marriage reflects Christ's relationship with the church. In marriage, a husband and wife are to sacrifice for one another in the same loving manner as Christ did for his bride, the church. As husbands and wives do this, their way of life is a testimony to the watching world of God's love for his people. As Pastor Harry Reeder said, "Foundationally, marriage is a blessing to humanity, and its primary purpose is to reveal God's redemptive covenantal relationship with his people."[89] Thus, the institution of marriage should be treasured and viewed with admiration.

Next, God gives us instructions on how to hold marriage in honor. Hebrews 13:4 states that the marriage bed should remain undefiled. For married couples, this means remaining sexually faithful to one's spouse. For those not married, it means not engaging in any sexual relations outside of marriage. As John Piper explains, "Both are a dishonor to marriage and a defiling of the marriage bed, because God made marriage, and marriage alone, as the one holy and safe and ultimately joyful place for sexual relations."[90]

---

89. Harry L. Reader III, "Honoring Marriage," *Tabletalk*, February 2019.
90. John Piper in a sermon titled "Let Marriage Be Held in Honor Among All," https://www.desiringgod.org/messages/let-marriage-be-held-in-honor-among-all.

Holding marriage in honor does not mean that one must get married. It also does not mean that if a person chooses to marry that they should do so at a young age. Regardless of one's marital status, holding marriage in honor involves having a holy reverence for the institution itself and abiding by the principles that God has ordained for it in Scripture.

Parting Reflection

Would you say that you truly revere the institution of marriage in principle and practice?

Parting Prayer

Lord, we thank you for marriage. Increase our view of this grace. Please help us to honor marriage by deepening our understanding of both your instructions in Scripture and our desire to be obedient.

Showing Partiality
by Dishonoring Others

———————— ⑉ ————————

My brothers and sisters, do you with your acts of favoritism really
believe in our glorious Lord Jesus Christ?

—JAMES 2:1

I'll never forget the strange sight one Sunday morning while walking into the church I attended as a youth. About 20 feet from the door, there was a large cardboard box with a person sleeping inside. My family and I, presumably like everyone else, walked by as we stared inquisitively. After the service began, a disheveled-looking man entered the sanctuary. However, it wasn't just an ordinary person. It was the pastor. With this stunt and no congregants inviting him into the service, this pastor wonderfully illustrated the sin of partiality that James describes in chapter two of his letter.

But how do we show partiality? It certainly involves showing favoritism to a person or group of people based on judgments that we make about them. James gives the example of paying special attention to wealthy churchgoers while neglecting those who are poor. Such behavior is condemned in part because it goes directly against God's character.[91] James adds, "But if you show partiality, you commit sin and are convicted by the law as transgressors" (2:9).

By reading James 2:1–13 closely, we can see how honor and shame are bound up in this sin of partiality. In James's example, the rich person is described as having a gold ring, fine clothing, and is implored, "Here's a good seat for you" (2:2–3 NIV). The first two descriptors signal high social status, being regarded as worthy of honorable treatment. A "good seat" is not simply one with favorable sightlines. Instead, they are offering a seat of honor.

———————

91. See Deuteronomy 10:17; Acts 10:34; Romans 2:1; Ephesians 6:9.

Conversely, the other person is described as poor, wearing shabby clothing, and is told "Stand there," or, "Sit at my feet." The first two descriptors signal a low social status. "Stand there" and "at my feet" refer to seats of disrepute. James diagnoses the situation, "But you have dishonored the poor" (2:6).

The issue is not that honor was shown to the rich person, but that a lack of honor was shown to the poor man. Thus, beyond mere favoritism, our partiality is apparent in whom we choose *not* to honor.

Parting Reflection

Thinking beyond James's example, who do you show honor to when gathered with other Christians? Do you give special attention to leaders or a certain group of individuals? Or is there anyone that you typically ignore? This coming Sunday, find someone who is "poor" (whether financially or socially) and in "shabby clothing" and show honor to them.

Parting Prayer

Lord, we praise you for being a God who shows no partiality. We thank you for bestowing honor on us, as we are all greatly unworthy. Spirit, convict us when we commit the sin of partiality by not honoring certain people. And then empower us to love them well.

Maligned for Following Christ

———————— ⑾⑾⑾ ————————

For the time that is past suffices for doing what the Gentiles want to do, living in sensuality, passions, drunkenness, orgies, drinking parties, and lawless idolatry. With respect to this they are surprised when you do not join them in the same flood of debauchery, and they malign you.

—1 PET. 4:3–4 ESV

I remember a conversation in my high school football locker room when multiple players were harassing a teammate. Why? Because he was sexually abstinent and a virgin. No true malice was involved as the guy was a good friend of everyone making the jokes. However, they still meant what they said. They intended for him to feel humiliated for his position, which they thought to be antiquated and simply odd. No doubt, he likely felt embarrassed at that moment. I learned years later that this guy is a Christian, which I'm sure was the impetus for his sexual abstinence. As far as I know, this friend held fast. Yet, many teenagers succumb to peer pressure and do things in life they otherwise wouldn't do in order to avoid feeling ashamed in front of their peers.

The typical Western ethic says that we can do whatever we want to do so long as we don't hurt anyone else. Or, as some say, "If I don't do what my heart wants to do, I'm not being true to myself." In view of Scripture, this way of thinking is baseless and flat-out wrong. In 1 Peter 4, the apostle teaches us that our desires were never meant to control our lives. Instead, we were created to submit and conform to God's will. As Peter says, we are to "live for the rest of [our] earthly life no longer by human desires but by the will of God" (1 Pet. 4:2).

Living for the will of God brings enmity with the world (John 15:18–19; James 4:4; 1 John 2:15–17). At the same time, those of the world, even our friends, will instinctively malign our ways of thinking. The world won't understand God's will on certain issues and will even think it foolish. As Peter says, "They are surprised when you do not join them in the same flood of

202

debauchery" (4:4 ESV). This surprise can then lead to us being maligned, defamed, and pressured to conform to the world's way of life. Humiliation and shame are powerful influences on a person's behavior. Yet, we must remember that man's judgment is not final and that we will all give an account to God (1 Pet. 4:5).

As Scripture often refrains, do not be surprised if others malign you for following Christ. While the world may seek to shame us, we must find our strength and joy in God alone. As we bear various trials, anchored by faith in Christ, we desire that our perseverance "may be found to result in praise and glory and honor when Jesus Christ is revealed" (1 Pet. 1:7).

Parting Reflection

Have you ever been maligned for following God's will? If so, were you able to stand fast through faith in Christ? If a Christian has never been maligned for their faith, what do you think that says about their way of life?

Parting Prayer

Jesus, thank you that you despised the shame of the cross (Heb. 12:2). You went before us and suffered in the flesh. And we praise you for giving us the Helper, whom you sent to us from the Father. Spirit, help us to follow your will in all circumstances and to set our hope fully on the grace that will be revealed to us at the revelation of Jesus Christ.

www.ingramcontent.com/pod-product-compliance
Lightning Source LLC
Chambersburg PA
CBHW071934090426
42740CB00011B/1695